FREE Test Taking Tips DVD Offer

To help us better serve you, we have developed a Test Taking Tips DVD that we would like to give you for FREE. **This DVD covers world-class test taking tips that you can use to be even more successful when you are taking your test.**

All that we ask is that you email us your feedback about your study guide. Please let us know what you thought about it – whether that is good, bad or indifferent.

To get your **FREE Test Taking Tips DVD**, email freedvd@studyguideteam.com with "FREE Test Taking Tips DVD" in the subject line and the following information in the body of the email:

   a. The title of your study guide.

   b. Your product rating on a scale of 1-5, with 5 being the highest rating.

   c. Your feedback about the study guide. What did you think of it?

   d. Your full name and shipping address to send your free DVD.

If you have any questions or concerns, please don't hesitate to contact us at freedvd@studyguideteam.com.

Thanks again!

GACE Early Childhood Education 001 & 002 Study Guide

Table of Contents

QUICK OVERVIEW 3
TEST-TAKING STRATEGIES 4
READING AND LANGUAGE ARTS 8
SOCIAL STUDIES 30
MATHEMATICS 41
SCIENCE 58
HEALTH AND PHYSICAL EDUCATION 68
THE ARTS 78
PRACTICE TEST 84
  READING AND ENGLISH LANGUAGE ARTS 84
  MATHEMATICS 88
  SOCIAL STUDIES 93
  SCIENCE 95
  HEALTH AND PHYSICAL EDUCATION 97
  THE ARTS 98
ANSWERS AND EXPLANATIONS 100
  READING AND ENGLISH LANGUAGE ARTS 100
  MATHEMATICS 105
  SOCIAL STUDIES 110
  SCIENCE 113
  HEALTH AND PHYSICAL EDUCATION 115
  THE ARTS 116

Quick Overview

As you draw closer to taking your exam, preparing becomes more and more important. Thankfully, you have this study guide to help you get ready. Use this guide to help keep your studying on track and refer to it often.

This study guide contains several key sections that will help you be successful on your exam. The guide contains tips for what you should do the night before and the day of the test. Also included are test-taking tips. Knowing the right information is not always enough. Many well-prepared test takers struggle with exams. These tips will help equip you to accurately read, assess, and answer test questions.

A large part of the guide is devoted to showing you what content to expect on the exam and to helping you better understand that content. Near the end of this guide is a practice test so that you can see how well you have grasped the content. Then, answers explanations are provided so that you can understand why you missed certain questions.

Don't try to cram the night before you take your exam. This is not a wise strategy for a few reasons. First, your retention of the information will be low. Your time would be better used by reviewing information you already know rather than trying to learn lots of new information. Second, you will likely become stressed as you try to gain large amount of knowledge in a short amount of time. Third, you will be depriving yourself of sleep. So be sure to go to bed at a reasonable time the night before. Being well-rested helps you focus and remain calm.

Be sure to eat a substantial breakfast the morning of the exam. If you are taking the exam in the afternoon, be sure to have a good lunch as well. Being hungry is distracting and can make it difficult to focus. You have hopefully spent lots of time preparing for the exam. Don't let an empty stomach get in the way of success!

When travelling to the testing center, leave earlier than needed. That way, you have a buffer in case you experience any delays. This will help you remain calm and will keep you from missing your appointment time at the testing center.

Be sure to pace yourself during the exam. Don't try to rush through the exam. There is no need to risk performing poorly on the exam just so you can leave the testing center early. Allow yourself to use all of the allotted time if needed.

Remain positive while taking the exam even if you feel like you are performing poorly. Thinking about the content you should have mastered will not help you perform better on the exam.

Once the exam is complete, take some time to relax. Even if you feel that you need to take the exam again, you will be well served by some down time before you begin studying again. It's often easier to convince yourself to study if you know that it will come with a reward!

Test-Taking Strategies

1. Predicting the Answer

When you feel confident in your preparation for a multiple-choice test, try predicting the answer before reading the answer choices. This is especially useful on questions that test objective factual knowledge or that ask you to fill in a blank. By predicting the answer before reading the available choices, you eliminate the possibility that you will be distracted or led astray by an incorrect answer choice. You will feel much more confident in your selection if you read the question, predict the answer, and then find your prediction among the answer choices. After using this strategy, be sure to still read all of the answer choices carefully and completely. If you feel unprepared, you should not attempt to predict the answers. This would be a waste of time and an opportunity for your mind to wander in the wrong direction.

2. Reading the Whole Question

Too often, test takers scan a multiple-choice question, recognize a few familiar words, and immediately jump to the answer choices. Test authors are aware of this common impatience, and they will sometimes prey upon it. For instance, a test author might subtly turn the question into a negative, or he or she might redirect the focus of the question right at the end. The only way to avoid falling into these traps is to read the entirety of the question carefully before reading the answer choices.

3. Looking for Wrong Answers

Long and complicated multiple-choice questions can be intimidating. One way to simplify a difficult multiple-choice question is to eliminate all of the answer choices that are clearly wrong. In most sets of answers, there will be at least one selection that can be dismissed right away. If the test is administered on paper, the test taker could draw a line through it to indicate that it may be ignored; otherwise, the test taker will have to perform this operation mentally or on scratch paper. In either case, once the obviously incorrect answers have been eliminated, the remaining choices may be considered. Sometimes identifying the clearly wrong answers will give the test taker some information about the correct answer. For instance, if one of the remaining answer choices is a direct opposite of one of the eliminated answer choices, it may well be the correct answer. The opposite of obviously wrong is obviously right! Of course, this is not always the case. Some answers are obviously incorrect simply because they are irrelevant to the question being asked. Still, identifying and eliminating some incorrect answer choices is a good way to simplify a multiple-choice question.

4. Don't Overanalyze

Anxious test takers often overanalyze questions. When you are nervous, your brain will often run wild causing you to make associations and discover clues that don't actually exist. If you feel that this may be a problem for you, do whatever you can to slow down during the test. Try taking a deep breath or counting to ten. As you read and consider the question, restrict yourself to the particular words used by the author. Avoid thought tangents about what the author *really* meant, or what he or she was *trying* to say. The only things that matter on a multiple-choice test are the words that are actually in the question. You must avoid reading too much into a multiple-choice question, or supposing that the writer meant something other than what he or she wrote.

5. No Need for Panic

It is wise to learn as many strategies as possible before taking a multiple-choice test, but it is likely that you will come across a few questions for which you simply don't know the answer. In this situation, avoid panicking. Because most multiple-choice tests include dozens of questions, the relative value of a single wrong answer is small. Moreover, your failure on one question has no effect on your success elsewhere on the test. As much as possible, you should compartmentalize each question on a multiple-choice test. In other words, you should not allow your feelings about one question to affect your success on the others. When you find a question that you either don't understand or don't know how to answer, just take a deep breath and do your best. Read the entire question slowly and carefully. Try rephrasing the question a couple of different ways. Then, read all of the answer choices carefully. After eliminating obviously wrong answers, make a selection and move on to the next question.

6. Confusing Answer Choices

When working on a difficult multiple-choice question, there may be a tendency to focus on the answer choices that are the easiest to understand. Many people, whether consciously or not, gravitate to the answer choices that require the least concentration, knowledge, and memory. This is a mistake. When you come across an answer choice that is confusing, you need to give it extra attention. A question might be confusing because you do not know the subject matter to which it refers. If this is the case, don't eliminate the answer before you have affirmatively settled on another. When you come across an answer choice of this type, set it aside as you look at the remaining choices. If you can confidently assert that one of the other choices is correct, you can leave the confusing answer aside. Otherwise, you will need to take a moment to try to better understand the confusing answer choice. Rephrasing is one way to tease out the sense of a confusing answer choice.

7. Your First Instinct

Many people struggle with multiple-choice tests because they overthink the questions. If you have studied sufficiently for the test, you should be prepared to trust your first instinct once you have carefully and completely read the question and all of the answer choices. There is a great deal of research to suggest that the mind can come to the correct conclusion very quickly once it has obtained all of the relevant information. At times, it may seem to you as if your intuition is working faster even than your reasoning mind. This may in fact be true. The knowledge you obtain while studying may be retrieved from your subconscious before you have a chance to work out the associations that support it. Verify your instinct by working out the reasons that it should be trusted.

8. Key Words

Many test takers struggle with multiple-choice questions because they have poor reading comprehension skills. Quickly reading and understanding a multiple-choice question requires a mixture of skill and experience. To help with this, try jotting down a few key words and phrases on a piece of scrap paper. Doing this concentrates the process of reading and forces the mind to weigh the relative importance of the question's parts. In selecting words and phrases to write down, the test taker thinks about the question more deeply and carefully. This is especially true for multiple-choice questions that are preceded by a long prompt.

9. Subtle Negatives

One of the oldest tricks in the multiple-choice test writer's book is to subtly reverse the meaning of a question with a word like *not* or *except*. If you are not paying attention to each word in the question, you can easily be led astray by this trick. For instance, a common question format is, "Which of the following is...?" Obviously, if the question instead is, "Which of the following is not....?," then the answer will be quite different. Even worse, the test makers are aware of the potential for this mistake and will include one answer choice that would be correct if the question were not negated or reversed. A test taker who misses the reversal will find what he or she believes to be a correct answer and will be so confident that he or she will fail to reread the question and discover the original error. The only way to avoid this is to practice a wide variety of multiple-choice questions and to pay close attention to each and every word.

10. Reading Every Answer Choice

It may seem obvious, but you should always read every one of the answer choices! Too many test takers fall into the habit of scanning the question and assuming that they understand the question because they recognize a few key words. From there, they pick the first answer choice that answers the question they believe they have read. Test takers who read all of the answer choices might discover that one of the latter answer choices is actually *more* correct. Moreover, reading all of the answer choices can remind you of facts related to the question that can help you arrive at the correct answer. Sometimes, a misstatement or incorrect detail in one of the latter answer choices will trigger your memory of the subject and will enable you to find the right answer. Failing to read all of the answer choices is like not reading all of the items on a restaurant menu. You might miss out on the perfect choice.

11. Spot the Hedges

One of the keys to success on multiple-choice tests is paying close attention to every word. This is never more true than with words like *almost*, *most*, *some*, and *sometimes*. These words are called "hedges", because they indicate that a statement is not totally true or not true in every place and time. An absolute statement will contain no hedges, but in many subjects, like literature and history, the answers are not always straightforward. There are always exceptions to the rules in these subjects. For this reason, you should favor those multiple-choice questions that contain hedging language. The presence of qualifying words indicates that the author is taking special care with his or her words, which is certainly important when composing the right answer. After all, there are many ways to be wrong, but there is only one way to be right! For this reason, it is wise when taking a multiple-choice test to avoid answers that are absolute. An absolute answer is one that says things are either all one way or all another. They often include words like *every*, *always*, *best*, and *never*. If you are taking a multiple-choice test in a subject that doesn't lend itself to absolute answers, be on your guard if you see any of these words.

12. Long Answers

In many subject areas, the answers are not simple. As already mentioned, the right answer often requires hedges. Another common feature of the answers to a complex or subjective question are qualifying clauses, which are groups of words that subtly modify the meaning of the sentence. If the question or answer choice describes a rule to which there are exceptions or the subject matter is complicated, ambiguous, or confusing, the correct answer will require many words in order to be expressed clearly and accurately. In essence, you should not be deterred by answer choices that seem excessively long. Oftentimes, the author of the text will not be able to write the correct answer without offering some qualifications and modifications. As a test taker, your job is to read the answer choices thoroughly and completely and to select the one that most accurately and precisely answers the question.

13. Restating to Understand

Sometimes, a question on a multiple-choice test is difficult not because of what it asks but because of how it is written. If this is the case, restate the question or answer choice in different words. This process serves a couple of important purposes. First, it forces you to concentrate on the core of the question. In order to rephrase the question accurately, you have to understand it well. Rephrasing the question will concentrate your mind on the key words and ideas. Second, it will present the information to your mind in a fresh way. This process may trigger your memory of some useful scrap of information picked up while studying.

14. True Statements

Sometimes an answer choice will be true in itself, but it does not answer the question. This is one of the main reasons why it is essential to read the question carefully and completely before proceeding to the answer choices. Too often, test takers skip ahead to the answer choices and look for true statements. Having found one of these, they are content to select it without reference to the question above. Obviously, this provides an easy way for test makers to play tricks. The savvy test taker will always read the entire question before turning to the answer choices. Then, having settled on a correct answer choice, he or she will refer to the original question and ensure that the selected answer is relevant. The mistake of choosing a correct-but-irrelevant answer choice is especially common on questions related to specific pieces of objective knowledge, like historical or scientific facts. A prepared test taker will have a wealth of factual knowledge at his or her disposal, but may be careless in its application.

15. No Patterns

One of the more dangerous ideas that circulate about multiple-choice tests is that the correct answers tend to fall into patterns. These erroneous ideas range from a belief that B and C are the most common right answers, to the idea that an unprepared test-taker should answer "A-B-A-C-A-D-A-B-A." It cannot be emphasized enough that pattern-seeking of this type is exactly the WRONG way to approach a multiple-choice test. To begin with, it is highly unlikely that the test maker will plot the correct answers according to some predetermined pattern. The questions are scrambled and delivered in a random order. Furthermore, even if the test maker was following a pattern in the assignation of correct answers, there is no reason why the test maker would know which pattern he or she was using. Any attempt to discern a pattern in the answer choices is a waste of time and a distraction from the real work of taking the test. A test taker would be much better served by extra preparation before the test than by reliance on a pattern in the answers.

Reading and Language Arts

Phonetics and the speech system

Phonetics is the study of the acoustical and articulatory characteristics of human speech sounds. The first major segment of the human anatomy that is involved in the production of phonemes, or speech sounds, is the subglottal system. This system consists of the structures below the glottis, the opening between the vocal folds. The subglottal system consists of the lungs, the diaphragm, and the trachea. The diaphragm is a muscle just below and attached to the lungs. Lowering the diaphragm fills the lungs with air, or inflates them; raising the diaphragm deflates the lungs, expelling air. Airflow through the nose, throat, and mouth is modified by various parts of the speech system to produce different sounds. Air from the lungs flows up through the airway called the trachea, commonly known as the "windpipe." It travels to the larynx or "voice box," which is found in the second major segment of the speech system.

The second major segment of the human speech system is the larynx, which is commonly known as the "voice box." It is located above the subglottal system, which is the first major anatomical segment of the human speech system. The larynx is composed of cartilage and located above the trachea, commonly called the "windpipe." Within the larynx are muscles known as the vocal folds or vocal cords. The vocal folds are attached at the front by the arytenoid cartilage to the larynx, but the opposite sides of the vocal folds are not attached to anything. The glottis is the space between the vocal folds. When the vocal folds are relaxed, the glottis is open and air flows through it with no resistance. This airflow produces devocalized, or voiceless, sounds. When the vocal folds are partially tensed, the glottis is partly open and the sound produced is a whisper. When the vocal folds are fully tensed, the airflow vibrates against the glottis, causing vocalization and producing voiced sounds.

The upper segment of the speech system is called the supraglottal system because it is located above the glottis, which is the opening between the vocal folds. The supraglottal system is made up of the pharynx, the nasal cavity, and the oral cavity. The pharynx is the region beginning above the larynx ("voice box") and ending below the uvula. The oral cavity contains structures that we use to produce different speech sounds, including the uvula, the velum, the tongue, the hard palate, the alveolar ridge, the teeth, and the lips. The uvula is the appendage of soft tissue hanging down from the top portion of the back of the throat. It is visible when looking at the throat through the mouth. The velum is the soft palate. The alveolar ridge is a line of hard cartilage just behind the upper teeth. People produce varying speech sounds partly by performing such manipulations as touching the tongue to the lips, teeth, alveolar ridge, hard palate, and/or velum.

Place of articulation

Relating to the production of speech sounds
Place of articulation refers to the area of the vocal tract whose shape is changed by speech-producing movements. These changes affect the size of the area through which air flows, varying the frequencies of speech sounds. The production of bilabial phonemes involves both lips touching and then then releasing, as in [b], [m] (voiced), and [p] (voiceless). The production of labiodental phonemes involves the upper teeth touching the lower lip and then releasing, as in [v] (voiced) and [f] (voiceless). Interdental phonemes are pronounced with the tongue between the teeth, as in [ð] (voiced "th" as in "the") and [θ] (voiceless "th" as in "theme"). Dental phonemes are produced by touching the tip of the tongue to the back of the front teeth. The phonemes [t] and [d] are pronounced dentally in some American English dialects (e.g., in Boston, Massachusetts and in Brooklyn, New York). These are, however, not examples of Standard English pronunciation. Alveolar phoneme pronunciation involves touching the tip of the tongue to the alveolar ridge, as in [t] and [s] (voiceless), and in [d], [z], [n], and [l].

Corresponding speech sounds they produce

Place of articulation refers to the location in the vocal tract that changes shape due to muscular movements, and thereby modifies the sound of the air flowing through the vocal tract. Pronouncing alveopalatal phonemes involves moving the tongue between the alveolar ridge and the hard palate, as in [ʃ]/"sh," [tʃ]/"ch" (voiceless), [ʒ] (as in "mea**s**ure" or "rou**g**e"), and [ʤ] [as in "judge" (voiced)]. Palatal phonemes are produced by moving the body of the tongue toward the hard palate, as in [j] (i.e. the sound of the "y" in "you"). Velar phonemes are produced by moving the body of the tongue toward the velum/soft palate, as in [k] (voiceless), [g], and [ŋ] ["-ng" (voiced)]. Uvular phonemes, made by moving the back of the tongue toward the uvula, are not found in English, but are used to produce the French "r" sound ([ʁ], which is voiced, and [x], which is voiceless). Pharyngeal phonemes, produced by articulating the root of the tongue toward the back of the pharynx, are not found in English, but are found in Hebrew, Arabic, and other similar languages. Glottal phonemes, produced at the vocal fold opening/glottis, include the English [h] and the glottal stop [ʔ].

Manner of articulation

Whereas place of articulation refers to the part of the vocal tract we alter to vary phonemes, manner of articulation refers to how the tongue and/or lips control airflow to vary phonemes. Producing plosives involves completely blocking airflow, and then releasing it, as in [p], [b], [t], [d], [k], and [g]. Producing fricatives involves partially blocking airflow, which causes vibration and produces hissing (devocalized) or buzzing (vocalized) sounds, such as [f], [v], [s], [z], [ʃ]/"sh," and [ʒ]/"zh." Affricates are combinations of plosives and fricatives or stops and vibrations, such as [tʃ]/"ch" and [ʤ], as in "judge." Nasals are produced by lowering the velum or soft palate and blocking the vocal tract so that air flows out through the nasal cavity instead of through the oral cavity. American English nasal consonants include [n], [m], and [ŋ]/"ng." While the other consonant phonemes discussed above may be vocalized/voiced or devocalized/voiceless, nasals are always vocalized. Approximants are formed by tightening the vocal tract without blocking airflow, as in [l], [r], [j] (the "y" sound), and [w].

Tap and trill

The tap is produced by quickly touching an articulator to and releasing it from some part of the vocal tract. For example, the tongue quickly touches the alveolar ridge and moves away from it to produce the medial/middle sound [ɾ] in the English words "better," "ladder," etc. The tap is also found in Spanish in short or unrolled "r" sounds. An example is the medial sound in the word *para* (which translates to "for" in English). The trill is produced by rapidly vibrating the tip of the tongue against the roof of the mouth. The trill, also known as a "rolled r," is used in British and Scottish English. It is also used in Spanish for long, trilled, or rolled r's, such as those found in words spelled with double r's. An example of this type of word is the Spanish word meaning "dog": *perro*. The trill is also found in words beginning with r, since initial r's in Spanish are commonly rolled. An example is the Spanish word meaning "rats": *ratones*. To American/English ears, this word sounds like "rrrrratones."

Classification of vowel phonemes

Vowel sounds are phonetically classified according to tongue height, tongue "backness," tension/laxity, and lip rounding/unrounding. The closer to the roof of the mouth the tongue is, the higher the vowel sound. In English, high vowels include [i] ("ee"), [I] as in "it," [u] as in "loot," and [U] as in "look." Middle-height vowels include [e] as in "ray," [E] as in "red," [O] as in "hole," and [ɔ] as in "haul." Low vowels include [a] as in "father" and [æ] as in "fat." Tongue "backness" refers to how far/near the tongue is from/to the back of the mouth. Front vowels include [i], [I], [e], [ɛ] as in "wet," and [æ]. Central vowels include [a] and [ə] (schwa), which is the sound of the "a" in "about." Back vowels include [u], [U], [O], and [ɔ]. Vowels using high articulator tension are classified as tense, and include [i] and [e]. Vowels using lower tension are classified as lax, and include [I] and [ɛ]. The lips can be rounded, as with the vowels [u] and [O]; or unrounded, as with [i] or [ɛ].

Phonological awareness, phonemic awareness, and phonics

Phonological awareness refers to the awareness of the sounds that make up a spoken language. This includes being aware of the fact that certain speech sounds rhyme with one another, and that it is possible to break down spoken sentences into individual words, words into individual syllables, and syllables into individual phonemes or speech sounds. Phonological awareness also includes the abilities to talk about speech sounds; to think about them; and to manipulate them into various combinations, sequences, and patterns. The latter includes changing one word into another by inserting, deleting, or exchanging an individual phoneme. Moreover, phonological awareness is an understanding of the relationship between spoken and written language. Typically, children's phonological awareness skills develop continuously and gradually throughout the later preschool years. Children develop phonological awareness through their exposure to language and through direct training, both of which are provided by the adults around them and in their lives.

Phonological awareness focuses on the awareness of speech sounds, which young children typically develop and learn before they learn to read. *Phonemic awareness* refers to awareness of the individual phonemes or speech sounds used in the child's native language, which the child hears in the language spoken by the adults and older children around them in their environment. *Phonological awareness* instruction teaches children to recognize the speech sounds they hear, to identify and differentiate these sounds, to produce them accurately, and to manipulate them. Good phonological awareness facilitates children's ability to make connections between sounds and alphabet letters, hence facilitating phonics. *Phonics* is the instructional method used to establish the Alphabetic Principle (i.e. the concept of sound-to-letter correspondence) and teach skills for decoding (breaking words down to their component sounds/letters) and encoding (blending/combining individual sounds/letters to form words).

Developing phonological and phonemic awareness skills
By developing phonological and phonemic awareness skills, young children develop awareness of the sounds used in their native language. Significantly, they also learn to make the association between the speech sounds (phonemes) they hear and the written/printed letter symbols that represent them. Understanding this connection gives young children the foundation they need for the development of future skills, including word recognition skills and the decoding skills needed to read printed/written language. When young children develop phonological and phonemic awareness, they are less likely to experience deficits or delays in learning to read, and are more likely to achieve success in reading and spelling. The consensus of a great deal of educational research is that strong phonological and phonemic awareness in children is often a predictor of future long-term success in spelling, reading, and overall literacy performance. Research has also found that this awareness is a more accurate predictor of future success than vocabulary knowledge, intelligence, socioeconomic status, and other related factors.

Skills that should be developed by the later part of early childhood
Young children who have developed phonological awareness can typically recognize the sounds of alliteration in spoken language, which is the repeated use of the same or similar consonants (e.g., "She sells seashells by the seashore"); the sounds of rhyming words; the sounds of words with the same initial sounds (e.g., "Wee Willie Winkie"); and final sounds. They can typically divide words into smaller parts, such as syllables and phonemes (speech sounds). They can usually also count these smaller parts. When given isolated speech sounds, they are typically able to blend these separate phonemes together to form familiar words. Children with good phonemic awareness realize that words are composed of phonemes, and that these individual

sounds are symbolically represented by written/printed letters. Hence, they understand the relationship between speech and writing/print. Phonologically aware preschool children can typically also manipulate spoken language by adding, removing, or substituting specific speech sounds to create different words.

Benefits from instruction designed to develop PPA

Phonological and phonemic awareness (PPA) instruction benefits all children learning to read, which includes preschoolers, kindergarteners, and first-graders. In addition, PPA instruction is important for children who are at risk for reading problems. Such children typically have fewer alphabetic skills due to less exposure to and less experience with using the alphabet. This can be because their families have less access to books and/or libraries; their parents have different expectations of reading, or they prioritize reading differently; or their parents do not realize the importance of reading aloud to children to literacy development. Preschoolers with delayed language development, who are more likely to be diagnosed with reading disorders by the time they reach school age, also benefit from PPA instruction. Enhanced PPA enables enhanced awareness of correct speech, so children with articulation disorders also benefit. According to research, children with spelling disorders perform poorly when given PPA tasks. Phonemic instruction improves their understanding of sound-to-letter relationships and their ability to recognize common spelling units found in words, thereby strengthening their spelling skills.

Oral language development

Because of the amount of variation among individual children in the process of normal oral language development, it is neither easy nor accurate to pin down any linguistic developmental milestone to a specific age. Therefore, ranges rather than ages are identified. For example, most normally developing children will utter their first recognizable words sometime between the ages of 12 months and 18 months. However, the progress of normal language acquisition is unpredictable in the individual child, a statement which holds true for other areas of normal growth and development. For example, one child may say his/her first word at the age of 10 months, while another child may begin using words at 20 months. The majority of typically developing children tend to begin speaking in complex sentences around the ages of four to four-and-a-half years. But again, because the pace of normal language development can vary, some children might use complex sentences by three years old, while others only develop this ability by five-and-a-half years old.

<u>Considerations for adults regarding young children's oral language development</u>
The vast majority of children's oral language develops with great natural efficiency. Adults need not try to force it, but can nurture it by providing language-rich environments. Practices that may help include talking to children regularly starting at birth; reading regularly to babies, toddlers, and preschoolers; naming objects, actions, and events children encounter for them; and playing games with speech sounds, words, rhymes, etc. Adults need not be concerned when younger children distort or substitute more difficult phonemes like /r/ and /s/ with easier ones; this is normal. However, if a child still mispronounces such sounds beyond the age of about eight or nine, hearing and speech testing and therapy are indicated. Newborn hearing screenings are vital, as hearing loss is the most common disability in infants. If a child seems not to hear others' speech, a child's closest family/friends have trouble understanding the child's speech, or a child's communication is obviously different from that of same-age peers, adults should consult hearing and speech language specialists.

<u>Genetic and environmental influences on oral language development</u>
As with so many other aspects of human growth and development, oral language development is a product of the combined influences of nature and nurture, and of the interactions between the two. Humans have inborn inclinations to seek out social interaction with other people. Babies communicate their needs and wants through crying and gesturing before acquiring spoken language, and they frequently understand adult communication. Researchers have pointed out

that social interactions and oral language development do not take place for the purpose of learning rules, but for connecting with others and making sense of the reality we experience. Children have inherent abilities to decipher linguistic rules through their environmental exposure to spoken language. They can do this without formal instruction. This is evidence of the influence of nature on oral language development, as is over-regularization. An example of the latter includes applying regular verb rules to irregular exceptions (e.g., "tooths," "freezed," "goed," etc.) until exceptions are learned. Adults' constant corrections during this learning stage are typically futile. In addition to natural and environmental influences, children's language development is also influenced by their own cognitive abilities.

<u>Guidelines for supporting the natural development of oral language skills</u>
Teachers should realize that whatever language and/or dialect a child speaks is a reflection of that child's family's and community's values, identity, and experiences. As such, it is a valid communication system that deserves respect. Adults should treat babies and young children as conversationalists even before they begin talking, because they learn conversational rules very early (e.g., attentive gazing, facial expressions, and turn-taking). A significant component of language development is peer learning, particularly in mixed-age child groups. Adults should encourage child interaction by providing activities conducive to talking and using a broad range of materials. Individual and collaborative activities should be balanced. Sharing books, building with blocks, engaging in dramatic play, and taking part in "shop"/carpentry-related activities all stimulate interaction and discussion. While peer learning is important, adults are children's main resources for initiating conversations, questioning, listening, responding, and maintaining language development. Adults should always keep this in mind. Continued interaction into the elementary grades and written language comprehension also support oral language development in children. Language informs all curriculum areas, so active learners in classrooms are always communicating.

Phonology, morphology, semantics, syntax, and pragmatics

Phonology is concerned with the rules for the combinations of speech sounds within a given language. For example, while some African languages include words beginning with the –ng/[ŋ] phoneme, in English this sound is only word-medial or word-final, never word-initial. Most speakers follow such rules unconsciously. Morphology focuses on the smallest structural/grammatical units that convey or affect meaning. For example, in books, the noun book and the plural –s ending are each morphemes. Semantics focuses on the meanings of morphemes, words, and sentences. Syntax refers to sentence structure and word order, and is related to a language's rules for correctly combining morphemes and words into suffixes/inflections, sentences, questions, imperatives, etc. For example, features like participial modifiers and the verbs they modify are placed in a different order in German and English. The verb-containing phrase "I walked" would follow modifiers like "happily," "down the street," and "on a sunny day" in German, but would precede most if not all modifiers in English. Pragmatics focuses on rules for using language appropriately in various situations. An example of pragmatics would be how to speak at home versus how to speak at school or work.

Common approaches to communicate with young children

Researchers have found that a common practice among teachers when they are using language in their classrooms is to use linear or one-way questions requiring linear/one-way responses. However, experts recommend using reciprocal instructional approaches (e.g., asking open-ended questions that enable two-way/three-way responses). Studies also reveal that teachers are likely to dominate the classroom verbally. Experts believe a better approach would be to encourage and elicit children's conversational language and higher order cognitive skills by deliberately incorporating these into children's play activities. Experts state that teachers should have someone record a video of them during children's play time so they can monitor their own verbal behavior. Teachers should note how many times they verbally describe what the children do, how many times they repeat what a child says and then add some further information to it, how often they comment on and describe the properties of objects, and how often they ask open-ended questions. They should reflect not only on the number and duration of verbal interactions, but also on the quality of each conversation.

Following the CAR teaching strategy

Some researchers recommend using a teaching strategy called "Following the CAR" to engage in conversations with two- to five-year-old children. The C in CAR stands for Comment. In this step, the adult should comment on what a child is looking at, handling, or talking about. The adult should then wait five seconds. Experts find that this interval is important because it gives the young child time to hear and cognitively process the adult's comment, experience a response, formulate that response into verbal form, and then express it orally. The A stands for Ask. To continue the conversation the adult has begun and/or to start a new one, the adult should then ask the child questions about something the child is looking at, handling, or talking about. The adult should again wait five seconds to give the child time to respond. The R stands for Respond. Once the child gives an oral response, the adult should respond to what the child says by repeating the child's response and then adding a bit more information to extend the child's knowledge.

Real conversations

Experts define "real" conversations as those that interest the child and consist of three to four exchanges/"turns" between the child and the adult. Having at least one real conversation with each child on a daily basis is a highly effective way to improve vocabulary development and develop listening comprehension beyond the level of individual words. Teaching strategies that support children's active participation in real conversations include the following: attentively listening to what the children say; inviting the children to join extended conversations with adults and peers; demonstrating genuine interest in and affection for the children; sending verbal and non-verbal messages that are consistent; avoiding making judgmental comments about children or anybody else to or in front of the children; addressing the children with courtesy; availing oneself of spontaneously occurring opportunities for informal conversations with each child, and/or even planning some opportunities; basing conversations on children's specific interests; and using children's experiences, as well as songs, stories, and books, as topics for conversation.

Stages of English as a second language

For ESL children, the first stage of second language acquisition is preproduction, which takes place during roughly the first six months of learning. Listening comprehension is minimal. The child does not speak in English, but can nod/shake the head "yes/no," draw pictures, and point at things. In the second, early production stage, which lasts from roughly six months to one year into learning, children have limited English comprehension. They can utter one- to two-word answers, essential words, familiar phrases, and present tense verbs. In the third, speech emergence stage, which lasts from about one to three years into learning, children comprehend English well. They can speak in simple sentences, but still make mistakes in pronunciation and grammar. They often misunderstand jokes in English. The fourth stage is intermediate fluency, which begins about three years into the language acquisition process and extends to about the fifth year. By this stage, children have attained excellent English listening comprehension, and do not make many grammatical errors. In the fifth, final stage of advanced fluency, children's English language proficiency is similar to that of a native English speaker. Children typically reach this stage between five and seven years after they start learning English.

Ways in which English as a second language instruction can be improved
Research in the early 1990s found that regardless of the type of bilingual education language programs used (e.g., early-exit, late-exit transitional, or immersion), teachers tended to ask ESL students questions requiring low levels of English language proficiency and lower-order cognitive skills. Teacher knowledge of what stages of second language acquisition students are in, as well as an awareness of the kinds of prompts and questions that are appropriate for each stage both enable teachers to approach children using suitable levels of discourse. Another advantage of knowing the stages is that teachers can assess students' content knowledge as well as their English language proficiency. A third benefit is that knowing language acquisition levels enables teachers to use what Vygotsky termed the zone of proximal development (ZPD), the gap between a learner's current capability and the next level of ability. Vygotsky found that the ZPD can be utilized by providing necessary temporary support—which Bruner called scaffolding—that is gradually withdrawn as students progress.

Stage-appropriate prompts
Children in the preproduction stage of ESL acquisition comprehend little English. They do not speak English, but can nod, point, and draw. Teachers can give prompts like "Where is...?" "Who has...?" "Show me the..." or "Circle the...." In the early production stage, children's comprehension is limited. They can give one- or two-word answers, use some important words and familiar phrases, and use verbs in present tense. Teachers can ask "Yes/No" and "Either/Or" questions and questions requiring short answers consisting of one or two words. They can also use lists and labels to access and expand vocabulary knowledge. In the speech emergence stage, comprehension improves and simple sentences emerge, albeit with grammatical and pronunciation errors. Teachers can now ask children "Why...?" "How...?" and "Explain..." questions, and can expect answers in the form of phrases or short sentences. In the intermediate fluency stage, when students have excellent comprehension and can use correct grammar more often, teachers can ask children more abstract questions like "What would happen if...?" or "Why do you think...?" During the advanced fluency stage, when students approach native proficiency, teachers can instruct students to retell stories and make decisions.

Scaffolding and the zone of proximal development (ZPD)
Scaffolding, a term coined by Jerome Bruner, involves temporarily providing the support a learner needs to accomplish tasks just above his/her current performance level (i.e. things s/he cannot do independently, but can achieve with assistance). Lev Vygotsky identified the ZPD as the gap between a learner's current ability and the next level. He found that providing scaffolding enables teachers to exploit the ZPD to enhance learning. Teachers can apply this concept to ESL language development through direct instruction, by asking challenging questions, and/or by modeling correct English pronunciation and grammar. For example, a student in the first, preproduction stage of second language acquisition is able to find things, point at objects, and circle pictures, and such tasks are stage appropriate. However, a teacher can promote higher development by providing scaffolding to support students in answering Yes/No questions and/or giving one-word answers. These are tasks associated with the second, early production stage. With teacher support, the student can move to a higher stage of ESL acquisition.

Conversational vs. academic English for ESL learners
Conversational English requires basic skills that are used in interpersonal communication in everyday life, including basic vocabulary, grammar, and pronunciation. Conversational English enables ESL students to comprehend and participate in informal conversations with adults and peers. ESL children generally develop it after living in English-speaking locations for about two years. Conversational English is not particularly difficult cognitively. Children with conversational English skills sound fluent to most people. They converse in English, understand teacher questions, and may even translate for parents. However, their conversational fluency is often not reflected in school homework and tests. Teachers and parents may wrongly assume a child is unmotivated/learning disabled/lazy, when the true reason for the child's academic underachievement is that he or she lacks a knowledge of more cognitively demanding academic

English (such as content specific vocabulary in math, science, etc.) and complex-compound sentence syntax. ESL students take at least five to seven years to become fluent in academic English, and take even longer when they lack native language literacy at the time they enroll in an English language school. To understand textbooks, solve word problems, write reports/papers, and develop the problem solving and critical thinking skills needed to comprehend and communicate abstract and novel concepts, students must master academic English.

Word walls
Young ESL children learn English vocabulary words by repeatedly singing the same familiar songs and chants, and by hearing the same stories many times. Such repetition is also favored by young children. While ESL children are involved in activities featuring repeated story readings, rhyme recitations, and/or singing, teachers can supplement these activities to enhance further vocabulary building by providing word walls. A word wall uses visuals to illustrate concepts represented by vocabulary words, as well as by related words. Key characteristics of vocabulary words and related words may also be shown. A word wall can also illustrate concepts like synonyms and subcategories. For example, a word wall for "Chicken Little," "The Little Red Hen," or another poultry-related story could have a picture of a chicken at the top labeled Chicken. Below it on the left might be several related pictures labeled with their names: Rooster, Hen, and Chick. Under the main chicken picture on the right could be several labeled pictures showing chicken characteristics (e.g., Feathers, Beak, and the Eggs that hens lay).

Input hypothesis (Krashen & Terrell)

Krashen and Terrell, who identified the stages of second language acquisition, posited the input hypothesis. This states that when an ESL learner in one stage of acquisition is given instructional input that includes some structures characteristic of the next stage of acquisition, and is also encouraged to use language reflective of that next, higher stage, the learner will advance to that next stage in listening and speaking. The input hypothesis is expressed as i + 1, where i represents the speaker's actual or current level (or stage) of second language acquisition, and i + 1 represents the speaker's potential second language development level. Teachers who know the stages of second language acquisition and the appropriate types of prompts to use for each stage can adapt their prompting so that students respond commensurately with their current stage of English language development and with the next higher stage at the same time.

Jane Hill's Word-MES formula

"Word-MES" is a mnemonic for the key steps in applying the stages of second language development to ESL instruction. Students in the preproduction stage need to learn English vocabulary Words. Teachers should focus on helping students learn and correctly apply basic vocabulary. For example, using the story of "Goldilocks and the Three Bears," teachers can teach words like house, bed, cereal, oatmeal, too, hot, cold, hard, and soft. When working with students in the early production stage, teachers should Model correct English usage. For example, if a child says "Goldie runned," the teacher can respond, "Yes, Goldilocks ran and ran." Teachers should not make explicit corrections. When working with children in the speech emergence stage, teachers can focus on Expanding spoken/written sentences. For example, if a child says, "Bed was too soft," the teacher can expand on this by saying, "Yes, the second bed was too soft," adding the correct article and specifying adjective. Teachers can help students in intermediate and advanced fluency stages to Sound like books by exposing them to words outside their repertoires, repeatedly reading familiar books and singing songs, and using supplementary word walls.

Articulation disorders

Articulation refers to the pronunciation of specific speech sounds and phonemes. Some phonemes are harder to produce than others. Therefore, it is normal for young children not to produce some sounds correctly until they reach a certain level of maturity. For example, children are around seven or eight on average before they can pronounce difficult phonemes like /r/ and /s/. Some children continue to distort, omit, or substitute a certain sound beyond the age norm. Speech therapy can help address these types of issues. If a child mispronounces multiple phonemes beyond the typical age ranges, testing is needed to determine the cause. Multiple factors can affect articulation, including hearing loss, misaligned teeth/jaws, missing teeth, a tongue that is shorter or longer than normal, velopharyngeal insufficiency interfering with complete vocal tract closure, breathing problems, mild cerebral palsy causing neuromuscular weakness and incoordination of the speech mechanisms, mild to moderate intellectual disabilities, and others. Some children's speech is difficult to understand due to multiple misarticulations, which may also be caused by any combination of the factors outlined above.

Aphasia

Aphasia is a language processing deficit caused by neurological damage or deficiency. It may be congenital or incurred during or after birth via accidental injury, including injury due to oxygen loss (hypoxia or anoxia). Two specific aphasia diagnoses are named after the scientists who identified them. Broca's aphasia has historically been thought to originate in the brain's left hemisphere, and Wernicke's aphasia in the right hemisphere. Recent research, though, suggests that both types involve more numerous, more extensive, and less lateralized damage sites in various locations. Broca's aphasia affects expressive language. A child with Broca's aphasia would exhibit difficulty finding/retrieving words and constructing grammatical spoken sentences at an age when fluent speech is normal. Wernicke's aphasia affects receptive language. A child with Wernicke's aphasia would have difficulty understanding what others say, and may learn to hide this through uttering stock phrases like "I'm fine; how are you?" and "You look pretty today."

Jargon-aphasia

Expressive aphasia and receptive aphasia may be somewhat more familiar to some people than jargon-aphasia. Expressive aphasia impairs an individual's ability to process, formulate, and produce spoken language. Receptive aphasia impairs an individual's ability to process, comprehend, and interpret others' spoken language. Jargon-aphasia is somewhat rare, and is often caused by traumatic brain injury. The injury appears to damage the individual's motor control and coordination of speech mechanisms. The person can mentally formulate thoughts using words, but cannot then express them orally. The patient typically cannot form words, but uncontrollably repeats syllables like "cacacacaca" or "nanananana" when he or she attempts to speak. In early childhood, this should not be confused with normal infant babbling. All babies repeat syllables. It is part of typical speech development. However, if a child is older (three to five years old, for example), cannot form spoken words, and only produces jargon babbling when he or she attempts to speak, speech language pathology and neurological evaluations are indicated.

Voice disorders

Voice disorders can affect various characteristics of a speaker's voice, such as tone, volume, pitch, and nasality. These types of disorders alter the voice's normal quality. For example, some children suffer from birth defects causing cleft lip and/or cleft palate. With the former, the upper lip is split vertically or diagonally, which is visually disfiguring and also interferes with normal speech production. With the latter, the palate or roof of the mouth is split on one or both sides. Causes include parental genetics; genetic and congenital syndromes; multiple birth defects; and prenatal exposure to viruses, drugs, or environmental toxins. Effects include feeding and speech difficulties, ear infections, nasal shape changes, misaligned teeth, and disfigurement. A common symptom of untreated cleft palate is hypernasal speech. Vocal abuse (e.g., excessive screaming/singing/talking) can create vocal cord nodules or polyps. These can result in a hoarse, breathy, or rough voice; reduced pitch range; throat/neck/ear-to-ear pain; and vocal and physical fatigue. Vocal cord paralysis can cause hoarseness/breathiness, vocalization limited to one second, inability to speak loudly/clearly, restricted wind, and choking/aspiration while eating/drinking.

Stuttering

Stuttering is often described by clinicians as a disorder of rate and rhythm. Stutterers may speak faster/slower than normal, or may alternately speed up and slow down their speech without using typical rhythm regulation in their sentences, questions, etc. Common stuttering symptoms include <u>repetitions</u> of individual phonemes ("T-t-t-t-today"), syllables ("To-to-to-to-today"), and/or words ("To-to-to-to do that"); <u>prolongations</u> of consonant or vowel phonemes ("Sssssssssnake" or "Wooooooooould you?"); and <u>blocks</u>, wherein the individual struggles so hard to produce the initial phoneme of a word that the tension causes complete airflow blockage. The individual's face will often turn red, and he or she may display accompanying learned behaviors like foot-stamping, fist-pounding, and/or facial contortions. Stuttering can be mild, moderate, or severe. Some mild stutterers are "fluent stutterers," demonstrating some repetitions and/or prolongations, but talking right through them without blocking. Some become adept at circumlocution, which describes the practice of "talking around" problematic initial phonemes/words using synonymous words/phrases. Theories of stuttering causes include delayed auditory feedback, which disrupts fluency because stutterers belatedly hear their own speech; anxiety with propositional speech; and lack of self-confidence. Some children simply "grow out of" stuttering.

Delayed language development

Some children develop skills for understanding and using spoken and written language significantly later than normal, even when individual variations are taken into account. This can be due to a number of causes. Children with mild or moderate intellectual disabilities are likely to show delayed language development as well as delayed cognitive development, as these are closely related. Some children do not test with obvious cognitive deficits, but may have minimal neurological damage, which can delay language development. Other children may have no organic basis for the delay, but have been born into environments where they are deprived of adequate environmental stimulation. For example, if a child's parents and/or caregivers/teachers do not routinely talk to them, have limited daily interactions with them, and never read to them, young children are likely to exhibit delayed language development. Some parents who do interact with and talk to their children may still be linguistically, educationally, and culturally deprived themselves. Their children may feel loved and have good self-esteem, but may have a level of language development that is below average for their age.

Alphabetic principle

The concept that written/printed letters and their patterns correspond to speech sounds is called the alphabetic principle. Children's future success with reading is strongly predicted by their early knowledge of the shapes and names of written/printed letters. Children's development of the abilities to view words as series of letters and to remember printed/written word forms is closely associated with their knowledge of letter names. Children cannot learn letter sounds or recognize words without knowing letter names. Being able to recognize and name multiple letters is a prerequisite for comprehending the alphabetic principle, which explains that spoken sounds and printed letters have predictable, systematic relationships. Children follow a sequence of first learning letter names, then learning letter shapes, and finally learning letter sounds. Singing the "ABC" song and reciting rhymes help children learn letter names. Playing with lettered blocks, large 3-D letters, and alphabet books helps them learn letter shapes. Teachers can plan informal instruction so that children are given multiple, varied opportunities to view, compare, and manipulate letters. Relevant activities may include identifying, naming, and writing upper-case and lower-case letters.

Not all children begin preschool or school with good alphabetic knowledge, which refers to an awareness that written letters represent spoken sounds. For those who have not developed this prerequisite skill, educators must provide well-organized instruction to enable students to identify, name, and write the letters of the alphabet. Once they master these skills, they will have the foundation necessary to learn letter sounds and word spellings. A general instructional plan revolving around the alphabetic principle includes several elements. First, teachers should give children explicit instruction in isolated letter-sound correspondences. Second, during each day's lessons and activities, teachers should give children opportunities to practice their developing knowledge of letter-sound relationships. Teachers should both review children's cumulative learning of letter-sound correspondences already taught and create opportunities for children to practice new letter-sound relationships they are just learning. Finally, to give students opportunities to apply their expanding knowledge of the alphabetic principle early and frequently, teachers can supply phonetic spellings of words with meanings familiar to children for them to read.

Pace and order of lessons

Teaching early literacy skills
There is no expert consensus regarding the speed or sequence that should be used to teach young children letter-to-sound relationships. However, educators generally agree that phonemes and letters with the highest utility—those used most often—should be taught earliest. These include m, a, t, s, p, and h. Conversely, x as in "box," gh as in "through," ey as in "they," and a as in "want" are letter-phoneme relationships that are used less frequently. The letter-sound relationships of consonants least subject to distorted articulation when pronounced in isolation should be taught first. These include f, m, and n. Word-initial or word-medial stops (p, b, t, d, k, and g) are more difficult for young children to combine with other sounds than continuous (fricative/affricate) phonemes are. Sounds that are easily confused (like /b/ and /v/) or letters that look similar (like b and d, or p and g) should be introduced to young children in separate lessons.

Sound-letter correspondences
Early childhood alphabetic principle instruction should be logical and consistent with the rates at which young children are able to learn. Teachers should introduce sound-to-letter relationships that will enable children to work with words as early as possible. According to research findings, direct and explicit instruction controlled by the teacher is more effective for teaching children the alphabetic principle than indirect and implicit methods are. Many teachers also use eclectic approaches, combining multiple teaching methods. Educators should remember that individual children normally learn sound-letter relationships at varying rates. A reasonable rate for introducing sound-letter relationships ranges from two to four relationships weekly. The earliest relationships teachers should introduce are high-utility ones. When introducing consonants and vowels, teachers should present them in an order that facilitates children's reading words readily. Teachers should avoid presenting similar-sounding phonemes and/or similar-looking letters together. They should use separate sessions/lessons to introduce single consonant sounds and consonant blends/clusters. Instruction in blending letters/sounds should use words with letter-sound relationships children have already learned.

Sound-to-alphabet letter relationships instruction

When a teacher is instructing preschoolers on the relationships between spoken sounds and written letters (known as the alphabetic principle), s/he might begin by introducing a few (e.g., two, three, or four) single consonant sounds and one or two short vowel sounds. Once the children have mastered these, the teacher can present some additional new single consonant sounds, present some additional new short vowel sounds, and introduce one long vowel sound in a subsequent lesson. Then, the teacher could introduce consonant blends like st-, cl-, etc. in a separate lesson. Another lesson after the one on consonant blends could focus on digraphs (e.g., ch, sh, and th), which would enable children to read frequently used words like "chair," "she," and "the." A later lesson could introduce consonant clusters such as str-, spl-, etc. Teachers should always teach young children single consonants and consonant blends/clusters in separate lessons to avoid confusion. .

English literacy development in ESL students

To teach ESL students to read English, teachers must know the essential elements of literacy development, the principles of second language acquisition, and the differing conventions of both the students' first (L1) and second (L2) languages. Second language acquisition is an ongoing, lifelong process. In many ways, the process of second language acquisition parallels that of first language acquisition. Regardless of their L1 or their formal L2 instruction, students demonstrate predictable error patterns in learning. Acquiring language is not a linear process. While formal instruction can expand knowledge and inform and ease the process of language acquisition, it cannot accelerate it. Therefore, it is also detrimental to require sequential mastery of each curriculum element before proceeding onto the next element. Activities using language that are meaningful to students within a relevant context and teacher guidance help develop L2 acquisition. Varying language conventions must be kept in mind during instruction. For example, letter-sound correspondences are more consistent in Spanish than in English. Spanish letters are pronounced the same way they are spelled, so Spanish-speaking children can find the multiple pronunciations of the same phoneme in English confusing.

Phonological differences between Spanish and English

Because letter-sound correspondences are more consistent in Spanish than in English, Spanish vowels have fewer possible pronunciations than English vowels. Spanish has fewer total vowel sounds than English, regardless of spelling. This makes learning English more complicated for Spanish-speaking children. In modern Spanish, the pronunciation for the consonants v and b is the same, but these letters have different pronunciations in English. Spanish and English both contain the phoneme /ð/. In Spanish, it is represented by the letter d; in English, it is represented by the letters th. In English, the consonant clusters /sk/, /sp/, and /st/ are word-initial, as in school, special, and star. In Spanish, they are always preceded by /e/, as in escuela (school), especial (special), and estrella (star). Spanish speakers thus have difficulty pronouncing such initial clusters, and often end up using Spanish conventions, saying "estart" for start, "espeak" for speak, etc. Some sounds exist in L2 but not in L1; some L1 sounds transfer to L2; and letter-sound correspondences may differ between languages. Therefore, phonological and phonemic awareness and oral language development are crucial for ELLs.

Phonemic focus of English literacy development vs. the syllabic focus of Spanish literacy development

In English literacy instruction with native English-speaking children, educators teach individual phonemes/speech sounds and their corresponding alphabetic letters (phonics instruction). Spanish, however, is a syllabic language, and Spanish reading is taught using syllables rather than single phonemes. Spanish instruction uses syllables to teach word spellings, word divisions, stressed/accented parts of a word, word reading, and simple sentence construction. English-speaking children are taught to "sound out" a new word they encounter while reading by separating it into individual letters representing individual sounds. Spanish-speaking children are taught to "sound out" words by separating them into their component syllables. For example, in English, children sound out "man" as /m/, /æ/, and /n/. In Spanish, children sound out manzana (apple) as man, za, and na. Teachers must realize that ELLs encounter many phonological, syntactic, and semantic differences between their first and second languages, and that children with less English proficiency depend more on L1 cues. ELLs also expend double the cognitive effort of native English speakers through their attention to new language sounds, meanings, and structures, as well as their attempts to learn new literacy concepts and skills.

Writing systems of different languages

Not only do different languages have phonological and orthographic differences, but they also use different writing systems. For example, although Spanish is syllabic in phonology and Spanish literacy instruction is syllabic, the Spanish writing system and letter-sound correspondences are (like English) alphabetic. The Chinese writing system is logographic. Rather than using alphabet letters to symbolize speech sounds, Chinese uses ideographs, or characters depicting concepts, to symbolize words. The Japanese language has a combined logographic and syllabic writing system. Directionality can differ, too. In English, Spanish, and other European-based languages, lines of writing/print go from left to right. In Hebrew, they go from right to left; in Chinese, they go from top to bottom. Therefore, children's ESL progress relies on their phonological awareness, their oral language knowledge, their grasp of the alphabetic principle, and their print awareness and book knowledge. These are best developed in purposeful contexts that are relevant to children.

Developing English language literacy

When teaching children learning English as a second language, teachers should make their instruction understandable to them. They can do this by providing visual aids, graphic organizers, and concrete examples of what they are teaching. They should consistently monitor children's language for development levels and use. They can paraphrase to clarify unfamiliar words and the concepts they describe. Teachers should take advantage of every opportunity to establish connections between children's L1 and English. They must repeat things frequently. They can also help ELLs by establishing a safe atmosphere where children receive ongoing support and feel comfortable taking risks. Teachers should adopt and communicate high learning expectations. They should enable children to develop necessary language and literacy skills that are consistent with their current levels of oral English proficiency. Literacy instruction should build upon children's comprehension, the alphabetic principle, and print concepts. Teachers should use language that children understand and find meaningful.

Instructing children to enhance their English language literacy development

Teachers should assess their students' specific needs, and then design instructional programs that address those needs. They should also design instructional plans expressly for new students. They should design instruction so children can understand it. They should assess student progress often. Based on data they collect through assessment and monitoring, teachers should make instructional decisions, including adjusting schedules accordingly. They should create plenty of opportunities for children to participate in extended conversations in English. Teachers should also seek out others in their preschool's community who have expertise in one or more areas, and should use these assets when creating their curriculum. ESL teaching strategies should be integrated into instruction in all content areas. Teachers should activate and access children's background knowledge and connect instructional content to children's real lives. They should give children opportunities to discuss learning materials, topics, and early texts. Teachers must also acknowledge and value diverse cultural patterns of speech and discourse.

Print awareness

Print awareness, also called print literacy, emerges gradually during the preschool years in normally developing children. Print awareness is the understanding that print conveys meaning, and the understanding of print's form and function. Research has found that children typically tend to develop print awareness between three and five years of age. Some researchers have observed that at this age, children go through a significant metamorphosis, wherein they demonstrate exponential increases in self-motivated, independent interactions with print. Such interactions include reciting the alphabet, identifying printed letters, recognizing printed words, and using print as a communicative mechanism. Many studies have concluded that the development of these print literacy skills by preschool-aged children is a strong predictor of their future achievement in reading. Studies have also shown that while four-year-olds have not mastered either word concepts or print concepts, they may acquire many print concepts sooner than word concepts.

Promoting literacy development and reading comprehension

Instructional strategies designed to promote early literacy development and reading comprehension that are used in many ECE programs (like the EC component of the Partners for Literacy [PfL] Curriculum) include interactive book reading, the 3N strategy, extended teaching, problem solving, and curriculum-embedded assessments. These are also suitable for teaching ESL children. Interactive book reading is a teaching method that should be used at least once per day with each child. Children participate either individually or in pairs. This interactive reading is done in addition to (not instead of) reading in large and small groups. The purpose of interactive book reading is to stimulate responsive, reciprocal instructional conversations between each child and the teacher. Interactive book reading employs three main component strategies: the 3S strategy (3S stands for see, show, and say), wh- questions, and expanded book reading.

3N strategy

In the 3N strategy, the 3 Ns are notice, nudge, and narrate. This teaching strategy involves providing scaffolding. Scaffolding is temporary support that helps a child advance from his or her current skill, knowledge, or competency level to a higher level. Scaffolding permits advancement that the child could not achieve on his or her own. The 3N teaching strategy can be employed to make any activity a learning experience for a young child, because it provides a structure for how teachers should interact with children. First, the teacher notices the level of an individual child's literacy skill(s). Second, the teacher verbally nudges the child to do things that are a step above his or her current skill level. Third, the teacher narrates what the child does, verbally describing and reflecting the child's activities. A number of literacy games designed for young children, including the Partners for Literacy curriculum's LiteracyGames, utilize a 3N instructional strategy.

3S strategy and wh- questions

Interactive book reading is a strategy aimed at generating responsive instructional conversations between the child and teacher. In the 3S strategy, the 3 S's are see, show, and say. First, the teacher asks the child to see/look at a specific feature in a book, such as the main character. If the child succeeds, the teacher then asks him/her to locate an image or a word on a page. If the child does this correctly, the teacher then asks the child to say a word/answer a question. This requires multiple responses, promoting children's attending behavior and building upon each student's abilities. During the say part of 3S, the teacher asks the child questions beginning with who, what, where, when, and why. These wh- questions help teachers assess children's listening and/or reading comprehension levels, and also encourage ongoing conversations between each child and the teacher.

Activities for expanded book reading instructional strategy

Expanded book reading is an instructional strategy that is part of the interactive book reading teaching format, which is used to promote early childhood literacy development. In expanded book reading, teachers can ask children to predict the possible subject matter of a book. They can give children an overview of a book. They can discuss setting, characters, and events in a book with children. They can help children relate the story in a book to their own lives, thereby making the book meaningful and relevant to children and helping them establish connections between literature and real life. Teachers can enhance the meaning of stories in books by acting them out using puppets and other props. To integrate literacy into all content areas across the curriculum, teachers can design math, science, art, and/or music activities that are related to a book students read. Teachers can ask children to retell the story they read together, which is an excellent way to informally assess their comprehension. This activity also assesses children's receptive and expressive language processing and speech-language production abilities.

Incorporating problem-solving strategies and skills

During each preschool day, teachers can help young children recognize their emotions, identify their own needs and wants, develop empathy for and identify with the emotions of others, recognize situations involving problems, come up with simple solutions to problems, and think about the potential consequences of problem solutions. These activities help children develop age appropriate and developmentally appropriate competencies for solving problems and making decisions. Periods of both formal and informal instruction afford opportunities for children to develop these skills. Developing problem-solving and decision-making skills at an early age has a number of benefits. Young children learn to self-regulate their emotions and behaviors through this development. They develop social skills for interacting with others. Moreover, developing early problem-solving and decision-making skills prepares children for the further development of the higher order cognitive skills they will need to succeed in formal primary, secondary, and higher education settings, as well as in everyday life.

Strategies helping to read new and/or difficult words

Phonics helps children read unknown/difficult words by teaching them how to sound out the phonemes represented by each printed letter. Teachers can help when children mispronounce words that have irregular spellings. They can also confirm children's correct pronunciations of words they have not heard or seen before. Context helps children deduce which of several possible words is most likely to be found in a particular sentence, paragraph, or book by examining its meaning in relation to the overall subject matter. Looking at a word's part of speech and how it fits into the sentence in question is also an example of using context. For example, reed and read have different spellings and meanings, but sound the same (homonyms). After reading the sentence "Reeds grow in marshes," a child knowing the meaning of "reads" can rule this word out even without knowing how it is spelled because it makes no sense in the context of the sentence. Children could also use their knowledge of language structure to analyze the sentence above. Children can ascertain whether a new word is a noun (person/place/thing) or a verb (action/state of being) by looking at its syntactic placement and its relation to the other words in the sentence that they are familiar with.

Formats used in children's literature and some genres

The picture book is both a genre and a format that encompasses various other genres. It includes wordless storybooks, which contain only pictures. Picture books integrate pictures and text to create a multimodal experience. Text is the most important feature of illustrated story books. Illustrations are secondary but complementary to the text. Poetry books contain poems rather than prose. Poems can use concrete verse, free verse, and rhymed and metered verse. Poetry emphasizes the sounds and meanings of words, and appeals to both readers' emotions and thoughts. Traditional literature is an adapted form of oral storytelling. It includes fairy tales, fables, folklore, epics, and proverbs. "Once upon a time…" introductions and happy endings are common features. Modern fantasy is based on traditional literature, but it is original. It includes modern fairy tales, such as those written by Lewis Carroll and Hans Christian Andersen. White's Charlotte's Web and Milne's Winnie the Pooh are also examples. Fantasy stories are imaginary, and often focus on good vs. evil conflicts, magic, and/or quests. Non-fiction informational books include narrative, how-to, question and answer, activity, life cycle, and concept texts.

Characteristics of good children's literature found in all genres

To select good children's literature, adults should determine whether a book tells an interesting story. The story should be age appropriate. It should also be appealing to a teacher's students. Books should be well-written, and should have original, believable, and well-constructed plots. Story characters should be credible and convincing, and they should grow and change as a result of their experiences. Dialogue should suit the characters, and should sound natural. Stories should have themes that are important to children. Adults should consider whether a book's theme is obviously moralistic. They should consider what the reader can expect based on a book's title and format. Illustrations should contribute to text, and vice versa. Good children's books avoid stereotypes based on race, gender, etc. They should afford pleasant reading/listening experiences. Adults can also read book reviews for guidance. Children's book authors should be knowledgeable about their subject matter, and they should write in a style suitable for the subject being discussed. Informational books should be accurate and well-organized..

Features of children's books that promote early childhood literacy development

Books that some EC educational experts refer to as "predictable books" contain repetitive text throughout. A salient characteristic of young children is their behavior of repeating familiar rhymes/songs/chants/phrases and stories over and over. Children find such repetition enjoyable. They also ask adults to read them the same books repeatedly. In addition to being enjoyable, repetition provides young children with opportunities to practice words and language patterns, and also encourages retention. Children also like repetitive books because they can immediately participate in the reading of the story. Some examples of good "predictable" children's books include the traditional stories "The Three Little Pigs" and "The Little Red Hen." Other examples are Dr. Seuss's "Green Eggs and Ham" and his story "What Was I Scared Of?" found in the compilation Yertle the Turtle. Another feature of children's books promoting early literacy development is pictures. Picture books with equal, interrelated/interdependent pictures and text help young children learn to recognize and begin to read letters and words by relating them to familiar visual images. The pictures in illustrated storybooks inform text, supporting beginning readers' continuing literacy development.

Abilities demonstrating phonological and phonemic awareness

Young children with phonological awareness recognize rhymes they hear, can rhyme words, can "count" the number of syllables in a word by clapping, and can identify words with matching initial sounds (e.g., "mother" and "milk"). Children with phonemic awareness can manipulate individual phonemes in words. For example, they can separate the word "cat" into the sounds /k/, /æ/, and /t/. Children who have problems with phonemic awareness frequently experience reading problems without early intervention. There are several issues teachers may observe in the classroom that can indicate phonological and/or phonemic awareness deficits. Children may not correctly combine individual phonemes to make a word. For example, they may not be able to select and blend the phonemes /k/, /æ/, and /t/ to make "cat." A child may not correctly perform phoneme substitution tasks to make different words. For example, a child may not be able to change the /k/ in "cat" to /m/ to make "mat." A child may have difficulty determining how many syllables are in a word like "paper." A child may also have problems rhyming, syllabicating, or spelling new words based on how they sound.

Word decoding and phonics

Word decoding ability consists of being aware of letter-sound correspondences and letter patterns, and applying them to correctly pronounce the words we read. Phonics is a reading instruction approach that focuses on letter-sound correspondences, exceptions to general rules, and strategies for sounding out new words. In the classroom, if a teacher observes a child is having trouble matching up letters with sounds (or vice versa), this can signal decoding and phonics problems that can interfere with a child's ability to read and spell. Children who can decode words, but must use a great deal of effort to do so, may have decoding and phonics problems. Difficulties with spelling words phonetically and reading are also signs of possible problems. Children who struggle greatly with phonics activities and patterns may have decoding deficits. Children who try to guess words based on the first one or two letters may have problems with decoding and phonics. If after teaching several letter sounds/patterns to a class, a teacher finds that certain children cannot recognize them while reading words and do not include these sounds and patterns in their writing, the teacher should suspect that these children are having problems with decoding and phonics.

Vocabulary frequently identified by educators

Educators frequently divide vocabulary into listening, speaking, reading, and writing vocabulary. These are not necessarily the same. Listening vocabulary refers to the words we must know to understand what we hear others say. Speaking vocabulary refers to the words we use when we talk. Reading vocabulary refers to the words we must know to comprehend what we read. Writing vocabulary refers to the words we use when we write. To read print, children must understand the majority of the words they encounter in a text. Children learn the majority of word meanings indirectly through daily life experiences. Well-designed instruction teaches them additional vocabulary. If a teacher observes that a child has more questions than usual about what words mean in age appropriate/developmentally appropriate texts, the child may have vocabulary issues. A teacher may observe that a child does not use or recognize many words compared to his or her peers, which could also indicate vocabulary issues. A child who cannot see connections/relationships among words in different texts may have vocabulary deficits. If a child frequently cannot find the correct word to express a thought, idea, etc., this could also indicate vocabulary difficulties.

Reading fluency

Reading fluency is the ability to read quickly, accurately, and smoothly both silently and aloud, and to read aloud with appropriate vocal intonations and expression. Children who do not read fluently sound awkward and choppy when they read aloud. Some students who read dysfluently have word decoding problems. Others simply need more reading practice to read quickly and smoothly. Reading fluency is important to children's reading motivation. When children find reading laborious or view it as a chore rather than an enjoyable experience, they dislike reading and avoid it. This exacerbates reading problems. Reading fluency becomes more important in upper elementary grades, when the volume of required reading increases exponentially for students. Therefore, younger children with poor reading fluency will also have difficulty meeting academic reading demands in the future. When teachers conduct correct words per minute assessments, children who do not meet the criteria for their grade level may have fluency issues. Struggling and becoming frustrated with speed and/or accuracy while reading aloud may indicate fluency problems. Reading aloud without expression is another sign of fluency issues, as are failing to pause at meaningful breaks in a sentence or a paragraph and failing to "chunk" words into meaningful units.

Abilities necessary for good reading comprehension

To have good reading comprehension, children must be able to (1) decode the words they read, (2) connect what they read to things they already know, and (3) think about what they have read in depth. Knowing enough word meanings (i.e. having enough vocabulary) plays a major role in reading comprehension. Children with good comprehension can make conclusions about what they read, including identifying factual elements, determining the causes of specific events, and identifying comedic characters. Therefore, comprehension involves a combination of reading, thinking, and reasoning. Teachers may observe a number of signs of reading comprehension problems. A child may focus on details/"trees" to the exclusion of the main point/"forest." This child can report how stories end, but cannot explain why. A child may not speculate about characters' motivations or upcoming events when reading a book. When trying to relate reading to his/her life, a child may choose irrelevant information. A child may not be able to recount logical event sequences in stories or isolate main facts in informational texts. A child may appear to have inadequate vocabulary to understand a text. Finally, a child may be unable to relate details of a story, such as the setting, what the characters look like, etc.

Reading components of phonological and phonemic awareness

The five basic reading components of phonological and phonemic awareness are word decoding, phonics, fluency, vocabulary, and comprehension. A deficit in any of these components can lead to reading problems. In addition to deficits in one or more of these areas, about two to three percent of children have central auditory processing disorders (CAPDs). Our ears receive environmental sound waves and convert them to acoustic impulses that are carried by nerves to the brain, which interprets these signals as various sounds, including speech. This is auditory processing. Children with CAPD have problems attending to, listening to, and remembering spoken information, and often take longer to process auditory input. They frequently cannot differentiate among sounds in words that sound similar to other phonemes, despite being able to hear them clearly. This causes decoding difficulties, which interferes with reading. Some children with strong auditory (and language) processing skills have deficits in phonological processing (i.e. processing phonemes/speech sounds specifically). This also typically causes decoding and hence reading difficulties. Language processing problems are broader, including deficiencies in linguistic experiences, vocabulary, comprehension (despite being able to correctly decode words), reading, and writing.

Memory

For children to read, understand what they read, and switch efficiently between the printed language they see and the information they have stored in their memories, children must be able to store information and retrieve it as it is needed. There are three main types of memory. Short-term memory holds small pieces of information for short periods of time. For example, when we hold a phone number in our mind only long enough to dial it, but do not retain it after it is dialed, we use our short-term memory. Working memory holds interim information in the mind for use during calculations. For example, we use our working memory when mentally multiplying double digit numerals or doing long division. Processing new information so that it can be stored for a long period of time, searching for stored information, and retrieving information as it is needed are also functions of working memory. Phonological working memory is a component of phonological processing that is important in reading comprehension, spelling, written expression, and retention. We store enormous amounts of information for many years in our long-term memory. This information influences our differential attention to various environmental factors and our perceptions of the world.

Dyslexia

Preschoolers/kindergarteners who have trouble learning alphabet letters are more likely to have trouble identifying sound-letter correspondences in first grade, and are more likely to have subsequent life-long difficulties with reading. Issues related to children's speech that can indicate dyslexia include mispronouncing unfamiliar, long, or complex words. This may include omitting word parts and/or arranging syllables or word parts in the wrong sequence. Other signs of dyslexia include speech that is not fluent (e.g., speech that is marked by frequent hesitations, "um's," and pauses); speech that uses vague or non-specific wording, such as "things" or "stuff," instead of correct nouns and names of specific objects; speech that suggests the child is having difficulty finding words while speaking, which is indicated when students confuse words that sound similar (e.g., substituting "volcano" for "tornado," substituting "humidity" for "humility," etc.); and speech that shows an inability to generate verbal responses to questions quickly and on demand. Students with dyslexia may also require more time than normal to respond orally to language stimuli; and may also have difficulties with rote memory (e.g., retaining and/or retrieving names, dates, phone numbers, random lists, and other isolated items contained in information presented verbally).

Dyslexic children typically show abnormally slow progress in their acquisition of reading skills. They often lack systematic strategies for reading new words (decoding, sounding out, etc.), and make wild guesses instead. Being unable to read short function words (e.g., "an," "on," and "that") is common, as is stumbling over multisyllabic words. Dyslexic children often miss parts of words when reading and/or fail to decode word parts, and may, for example, read a word aloud with its middle syllable missing (e.g., "imation" for "imagination"). Children with dyslexia tend to fear and hence avoid oral reading because they have made errors in the past and have an expectation that they will make additional errors if they attempt to read aloud again. When they do read aloud, they may omit appropriate inflections; sound like they are reading a foreign language; sound laborious and choppy, rather than fluent and smooth; mispronounce numerous words; and make numerous omissions and substitutions. While reading, they depend on the context to comprehend meaning, and have more difficulty understanding single/isolated words. Their performance on objective (e.g., multiple choice) tests is typically much poorer than their intelligence and knowledge would predict.

Children who consistently cannot complete written tests in the time allowed may have dyslexia. Children who cannot pronounce more difficult printed words and substitute easier ones for them instead (e.g., "car" for "automobile") may have dyslexia. In math, dyslexia causes difficulty reading word problems. Dyslexic children often misspell words. The spellings are not phonetic, but are often bizarre and wildly different from actual spellings and from native language conventions. Children with dyslexia read very slowly, finding it laborious and exhausting. Reading is such a chore to dyslexic children that they do not enjoy it, do not read for pleasure, and will avoid reading whenever possible. Such children have a lot of trouble learning foreign languages. Despite good fine motor skills and word processing abilities, they often have poor handwriting. Homework seems to take forever for dyslexics. Some students ask parents to read so they don't have to. Dyslexics' reading becomes more accurate with time and practice, but still remains labored and dysfluent. Dyslexic children often have family histories of problems with reading, spelling, and learning foreign languages. Dyslexia can cause low self-esteem. This is not always obvious, but can be detected by sensitive, skilled professionals.

Learning to spell

Children must understand the alphabetic principle—the concept that words are comprised of individual phonemes/speech sounds, and that the letters of our alphabet represent those sounds in writing/print—in order to learn how to spell. They must also develop a knowledge of specific letter-to-sound correspondences. As children gain more experience hearing, understanding, and using words, they start to observe patterns in the ways in which letters are combined. They also notice repeated series of letters that create syllables, common roots for many related words, prefixes, suffixes, word endings, and other word features. When children know these basic patterns and have also learned their language's basic spelling principles and rules, they can usually figure out how to spell new words they hear. Moreover, children can usually read words that they can spell. Therefore, children's development of good spelling skills promotes the development of good reading and writing skills as well.

Stages (Gentry, 1982) of children's spelling development

(1) Precommunicative stage: Children use alphabet letters, but may not know the whole alphabet, may not differentiate between upper case and lower case letters, or may not know that English is written from left to right. They do not demonstrate knowledge of letter-to-sound correspondences. (2) Semiphonetic stage: Children begin to comprehend letter-to-sound correspondences. They frequently use simple logic to symbolize words with single letters. A good example is using "U" for "you" (early texting potential!). (3) Phonetic stage: Children use letters to represent all speech sounds they hear in words. These representations may not always be correct, but are systematic and understandable (e.g., writing "kom" instead of "come"). (4) Transitional stage: Children begin the transition from phonetically spelling words according to their sounds to visually and structurally learning conventional word spellings. They still make errors as they assimilate this new knowledge (e.g., writing "highked" instead of "hiked"). (5) Correct stage: Children know fundamental English orthographic rules, including silent letters, irregular and alternative spellings, prefixes, suffixes, and other word features. They have learned many word spellings, and recognize misspellings. Their knowledge of exceptions to spelling rules and the generalizations they make about spelling are usually correct.

Invented spelling

When young children have not yet learned how to spell many (or any) words, they commonly "invent" spellings for spoken words they hear. They do this by identifying letters that correspond to the separate phonemes (speech sounds) they hear and arranging them in a sequence that matches the word's sounds. Linguistic researchers (e.g., Read, 1975) studying preschoolers have found that different children choose the same phonetic spellings. These children have developed phonemic and phonetic awareness, enabling them to invent spellings before they have actually learned to spell. This skill is a prerequisite to learning how to read, spell, and write. Researchers observe that neither adult influence nor chance could explain diverse children's high incidence of selecting the same phonetic spellings. Therefore, even at young ages, children can identify the phonetic properties of English words that are symbolized by their real spellings. Experts conclude from these observations that spelling is a developmental process rather than merely a word memorization process, and that it results in comprehension that goes beyond understanding simple sound-to-letter correspondences.

Writing skills development

(1) <u>Scribbling and drawing:</u> Young children grasp crayons/pencils with their fists, exploring form, space, and line. As their fine motor skills and cognitive understanding of symbolic representation develop concurrently, they progress to (2) <u>letter-like forms and shapes</u>. They comprehend that written symbols represent meanings. They start including shapes like circles and squares into their drawing and writing, but they are randomly located without much spatial orientation. Children in this stage commonly write figures and ask parents, "What does this say?" (3) <u>Letters:</u> Children can form letters, and start writing them randomly. They usually write consonants first. They do not initially possess a knowledge of symbol-to-sound correspondence; this develops gradually. Children tend to favor writing their own initials. (4) <u>Letters and spaces:</u> Children realize that printed/written words are separated by spaces, develop an understanding of the concept of a word, use 1:1 word correspondence, and write correctly spaced words. They write initial and final word sounds and vowels, correct the spelling of some high frequency words, and experiment with sentence construction and punctuation. (5) <u>Conventional writing and spelling:</u> Children write, spell, and punctuate correctly most of the time. They view various forms of purposeful writing as more important.

<u>Writing relative to purposes, audiences, and other aspects</u>
According to the National Institute for Literacy, writing is defined as "the ability to compose text effectively for various purposes and audiences." We use writing as a tool to help us collect detailed information, document it, and disseminate it to widespread audiences. We use writing to express our ideas, thoughts, and feelings, and to persuade our readers to believe or agree with what we write. Researchers have also found that the learning capacity of an individual increases when his or her writing skills improve. This aspect of writing skills mirrors that of reading skills in that the development of both improves learning ability. Students need instruction to learn to write well. Reading skills have been found both to be reinforced by and to reinforce important writing skills like spelling and grammar. Thus, when teachers help children improve their writing, they are contributing to the improvement of their reading abilities as well.

POWER strategy

One popular model of the writing process proposed by experts, the POWER strategy, has five steps. In (1) planning, student and teacher ask and select Yes/No on a checklist to decide whether the student selected a good topic, researched/read about the topic, considered what information readers would want to know, and wrote down all of his/her ideas. In (2) organization, the student and teacher ascertain if the student grouped similar ideas together, selected the best ideas for the composition, and arranged the ideas in a logical sequence. In (3) writing, the student and teacher decide whether the student wrote down his/her ideas in sentences. They also decide whether the student did his/her best to get help when it was required. To get the necessary information and assistance, the student may have consulted a text, asked a learning partner/classmate for assistance, and/or asked the teacher for help. In (4) editing, the student and teacher consider whether the student read his/her first draft to himself/herself, marked the parts s/he liked and those that might need changing, read the first draft to his/her partner/classmate, and listened to the other student's input. In (5) rewriting, the student and teacher look at whether the student made changes in his/her composition, edited it for correct mechanics, and wrote the final draft using his/her best handwriting.

Rating a child's early writing efforts to assess emerging writing skills

One easy rating scale (Clay, 1993) focuses on three areas: language level, message quality, and directional principles. Each category has six progressive levels. For language level, the categories are (1) alphabetical (writes letters), (2) word (writes any recognizable word), (3) word group (writes any two-word phrase), (4) sentence (writes any simple sentence), (5) punctuated story (writes two or more related sentences), and (6) paragraphed story (includes two themes). The levels for message quality are as follows: (1) Student has a concept of signs/symbols. (2) Student has a concept that a message is communicated. (3) Student copies a message. (4) Student repeats sentence patterns like "This is a…" (5) Student tries to record his/her own ideas in writing. (6) Student writes a successful composition. The levels for directional principles are as follows: (1) Student does not demonstrate knowledge of directionality. (2) Student exhibits partial directional knowledge (e.g., left to right or start at the top left or return from top right down to the left). (3) Student reverses the direction. (4) Student follows the correct directional pattern. (5) Student uses correct directionality and spacing between words. (6) The student writes extensively without problems related to arranging and spacing text.

Standard conventions of written English

Written English should meet the standard conventions of correct spelling, capitalization, punctuation, grammar, and handwriting. Traditionally, teachers have paid more attention to a composition's appearance, length, word usage, and spelling than to how well-organized it is or how appropriate its content is. This habit can cause a superficial focus on imperfect form, while essentially ignoring the fact that the function is effective and meaningful. Other readers also form negative first impressions of writing when its appearance and/or format are less than acceptable, even if it otherwise effectively conveys its message. One type of common spelling error is vowel combination reversals (e.g., writing "siad" instead of "said," writing "freind" instead of "friend," etc.). Capitalization errors include failing to capitalize words at the start of sentences, months of the year, and proper nouns/names. Another type of capitalization error is incorrectly capitalizing words/letters within words. Punctuation errors include omitting commas in dates, omitting commas before conjunctions in compound sentences, omitting/substituting semicolons in complex sentences, and adding extraneous punctuation marks. Grammatical errors include incorrect/conflicting verb tenses, subject-verb disagreement, missing articles, misplaced modifiers, and dangling participles. Handwriting errors/problems include illegible writing, poor alignment, and incorrect/poor spacing.

Motivating young children to write

Experts note that like adults, children prefer participating in activities they find exciting rather than ones they find unexciting/uninteresting. To motivate students to write, teachers can share personal journals and other samples of their own writing, post e-mailed/handwritten letters/notes in classrooms, display favorite magazines and books, and show children fun greeting cards/invitations. They should also invite children to bring writing samples from home. Teachers can create classroom "writing corners" that contain varied writing examples contributed by children and teachers. Diverse writing activities help children stay enthusiastic about writing. Children can take turns contributing a sentence for a daily class newsletter/journal/newspaper, and teachers can have students practice sounding out and spelling words as they dictate their sentences. Teachers can deliberately make some transcribing errors and have children correct them. Daily pages can be compiled into monthly class books. Connecting writing subjects to people/things that are familiar and exciting to children, and guiding students in how to write and ask classmates "interview" questions using modeling and other techniques both help motivate students. Encouraging/guiding children to evaluate and record their comments about authors, illustrators, and books can also be a motivational tool. Ultimately, children will learn to write their own critiques.

Social Studies

Levels of self-awareness

Even newborns demonstrate differentiation of body through rooting and orienting responses, which are triggered by touching the cheek. (1) Differentiation: At this level, children recognize correspondence between their movements and those in the mirror, and differentiate their mirror images from other individuals. They differentiate the self. (2) Situation: At this level, beyond matching the surface properties of what they feel and what they see in the mirror, and beyond differentiating the self, children realize that their reflection is unique to their self. They also realize that their body/self and other things are situated in space. (3) Identification: At this level, beyond differentiating and situating the self, children now identify their reflection as "me." When psychologists place a dot/sticky note on a child's face before s/he looks in a mirror, the child reaches toward his or her own face to touch/remove it, demonstrating self-recognition and an emerging self-concept. (4) Permanence: At this level, children identify a permanent self across time and space, recognizing themselves in photos and home movies regardless of year/age/clothing/location/setting, etc. (5) Self-consciousness/"meta" self-awareness: At this level, children recognize their self from others' perceptions/perspectives as well as their own. They experience pride, shame, and other "self-conscious" feelings.

Highlights in the progression of children's self-awareness

From birth, infants differentiate their bodies from the environment, and differentiate internal from external stimuli (i.e. self-touch/stimulation vs. non-self/others' touch/stimulation). From two months old, babies show a sense of their body's position relative to other things in their environment. They systematically imitate others' facial expressions and movements. They also explore and consider the environment's responses to their own actions. Additionally, they smile and socially interact face-to-face with others, showing a new sense of shared experiences. By four months, infants systematically reach for and touch objects they see, showing hand-eye coordination. From four to six months, they regulate their reaching based on their sitting/posture and balance. By six months, babies can differentiate video of themselves from that of other, identically dressed babies. Babies between the ages of four and seven months can differentiate live video of themselves from that of experimenters imitating the same behaviors. By two years, children develop an understanding of symbolic representation, and know that mirror images and pictures of themselves stand for themselves. They also start to develop language skills and develop the ability to engage in pretend play.

Contributing factors to children's early development of interpersonal relationships

(1) The first basic factor that contributes to the development of interpersonal relationships in early childhood is child-adult relationships. These are the earliest interpersonal interactions, and start to develop at birth. When children's needs are consistently met by adults, children learn to trust adults. In his famous theory of development, Erikson called the first stage of psychosocial development and the central conflict of infancy basic trust vs. mistrust. (2) The second factor is autonomy, which refers to making decisions and doing things for oneself. Toddlers develop autonomy. Erikson called his second stage of psychosocial development and the central conflict of toddlerhood autonomy vs. shame and self-doubt. Children who are consistently given developmentally appropriate autonomy are more likely to respect others' autonomy, a key feature of interpersonal development. (3) The third basic factor is pretend play, which emerges as children's understanding of symbolic representation develops and they begin to use things to stand for other things. Pretending to be grown-ups engaging in adult activities helps children learn about adult skills and roles. Interacting with peers in make-believe scenarios prepares children for real-life adult interactions. Constructive ECE approaches do not involve punishing children who have not developed sufficient interpersonal relationship awareness. Instead, they encourage adults to teach children socially acceptable behaviors and reward positive interpersonal interactions.

Developmental milestones

By the time they are a year old, most babies have begun to interact with their peers, particularly when it comes to activities involving concrete objects. The development of walking and talking abilities in normally developing toddlers by the time they are two years old enables them to coordinate their behavior when playing with peers. They can imitate one another's behaviors, and can alternate roles during play, as they understand symbolic representation and can create make-believe scenarios. Pretend play increases from the ages of three to five years, as do prosocial behaviors, which include helping and caring for others. At the same time, egocentrism and aggressive behaviors decrease, as children are more able to consider others' viewpoints and feelings. Emergent social interaction skills such as these form the foundation for children's early peer relationships. When children demonstrate preferences for certain peers and choose to play and otherwise interact with them over others, this is the beginning of what will develop into preschool friendships, which are based mostly upon mutual play activities and exchanges of concrete things. Children tend to form daycare friendships with members of their own sex only over time.

ECE views regarding conflict resolution processes

ECE experts find that while many elementary and secondary schools have implemented conflict resolution programs, children should start learning how to resolve conflicts at younger ages. For example, experts associated with the successful HighScope EC curriculum have designed an approach to conflict resolution for children from 18 months to six years old. The steps in EC conflict resolution are similar to those used to resolve adult conflicts in education, law, labor relations, and diplomacy. Such problem solving steps have also been found to be effective in daycares, Head Start programs, preschools, nursery schools, and kindergartens. While the steps are the same regardless of the age of the children, they are applied differently according to children's developmental levels. Adults supply much of the language to describe problems and solutions for toddlers; preschoolers can often do this themselves. After experiencing the conflict resolution process, elementary school students can frequently function as mediators for classmates. Even very young children with limited language skills should be encouraged to agree and participate through nodding, pointing, and answering yes/no questions. Conflict mediation and resolution skills help children develop lifelong problem solving and social skills.

The steps used to mediate EC conflicts resemble the steps used in adult mediation. For example, EC experts at the HighScope Educational Research Foundation designed a conflict resolution approach for children aged 18 months to 6 years that consists of these six steps: (1) Calmly approach the children who are in conflict and stop any harmful behaviors. (2) Acknowledge what the children are feeling. (3) Collect information about the conflict. (4) Restate what the problem is. (5) Ask children to suggest possible solutions, and help them choose one together. (6) Follow up by providing support as needed. Experts find that children as young as 18 months demonstrate emergent problem solving skills. They observed young children's abilities to immediately and honestly express emotions. They noted that with adult support, children can frequently generate simple and creative problem solutions. While school conflict resolution is typically aimed at preventing violence, teaching conflict resolution skills can also help children develop the social skills needed to grow into independent, productive members of society.

Parenting styles identified by psychologists

Psychologists (Baumrind, 1967; Maccoby & Martin, 1983) have identified four parenting styles: (1) <u>Authoritarian</u> These parents are strict, punitive, demanding, and unresponsive. They do not explain reasons for their rules to children. Their children are obedient and proficient at completing academic/technical tasks, but they are less competent socially and less happy. They also have lower self-esteem. (2) <u>Authoritative</u> This is the ideal parenting style. These parents are responsive, nurturing, and forgiving. They are assertive without being restrictive or intrusive. They set rules, but explain them. They are democratic, address children's questions and input, and use supportive rather than punitive discipline. Their children tend to be competent, successful, and happy. (3) Permissive These parents are indulgent, lenient, nontraditional, and undemanding. They are nurturing, responsive, and communicative with children, but do not expect their children to show much maturity and/or self-control. They avoid confrontation and seldom use discipline, often acting more like friends than parents. Their children's self-regulation skills are deficient and they are not as happy as many of their peers. They tend to have difficulty with authority and perform poorly in school. (4) Uninvolved These parents are undemanding, unresponsive, and uncommunicative. They meet their children's basic needs, but are relatively detached from their children's lives. In extreme cases, these parents may neglect/reject children. Their children have low self-esteem and lack self-control.

Family systems theory

Family systems theory studies the behavior of the family unit rather than the behavior of individual family members. Family behavior includes the interactions among family members and how the family unit responds to stress. Some family characteristics have been identified as particularly pertinent to ECE (Christian/NAEYC, 2006). They are boundaries, roles, rules, hierarchy, climate, and equilibrium. Hierarchy is a family's balance of power, control, and decision making. Culture, religion, age, gender, and economic status influence the family hierarchy, which shifts whenever changes occur in the family's composition. Climate refers to a family's emotional quality, and includes the physical and emotional environments in which families raise children. These environments reflect a family's belief about families and children. Family climate determines whether a child feels safe/loved/supported or frightened/rejected/unhappy in his/her family. Equilibrium refers to the family's balance and consistency. It is disrupted by stress and change, and is maintained or protected by family traditions, customs, and rituals.

Family systems theory examines not individual behavior but family behavior, including communication, interaction, connection/separation, loyalty/autonomy, and responses to stress within the context of the family unit. Family system components particularly influential in early childhood development include the following: (1) Boundaries This refers to limits, separateness, and togetherness (i.e. what/whom the family includes/excludes). "Disengaged" families value independence over belonging, and are open to new input. "Enmeshed" families value togetherness over autonomy, and have more closed/restrictive boundaries. (2) Roles Each family member has a role (e.g., helper, clown, peacemaker, victim, rescuer, etc.). Family members also tend to assume these roles in social, school, and work contexts. (3) Rules Family interaction rules have long-term influences (e.g., parents who view life as predictable are likely to plan ahead, while those who view life as less controllable may not prevent/avoid problems, but rather address them as they occur). Family rules can be unspoken. Also, the rules of family cultures and school cultures can conflict. The other three of the six prominent influences on EC are hierarchy, climate, and equilibrium.

Human socialization

Socialization is the process by which individuals learn their society's norms, values, beliefs, and attitudes; and what behaviors society expects of them relative to those parameters. This learning is imparted by agencies of socialization. The family, peer groups, and leaders of opinion are considered primary socializing agencies. The family is probably the most important because it has the most significant influence on individual development. Families influence the self-concept, feelings, attitudes, and behaviors of each individual member. As children grow, they encounter peer groups throughout life, which also establish norms and values to which individual group members conform. Schools, workplaces, religions, and mass media are considered secondary socializing agencies. Schools dictate additional academic and behavioral norms, values, beliefs, and behaviors. Workplaces have their own cultures that continue, modify, and/or add to the values and behaviors expected of their members. Religions also regulate members' behavior through beliefs, values, goals, and norms that reflect moral principles within a society. Mass media communicate societal conventions (e.g., fashion/style), which enables individuals to learn and adopt new behaviors and/or lifestyles.

Institutions that function as socializing agents

Family is the first and most important socializing agent. Infants learn behavioral patterns from mothers. Their primary socialization is enabled through such early behaviors as nursing, smiling, and toddling. Babies soon interact with other family members. All the infant's physiological and psychological needs are met within the family. Babies learn their sleeping, eating, and toileting habits within the family environment. Babies' personalities also develop based on their early experiences, especially the amounts and types of parental love and affection they receive. School is also a critical socializing agent. Children extend family relationships to society when they go to school. Cognitive and social school experiences develop children's knowledge, skills, beliefs, interests, attitudes, and customs, and help determine the roles children will play when they become adults. In addition to family relationships, receiving reinforcements at school and observing and imitating teachers influence personality development. Peer groups that are based on friendships, shared ideas, and common interests in music, sports, etc. teach children/teens about conforming to rules and being rejected for not complying with these rules. Mass media like TV profoundly influence children, both negatively and positively.

Culture

While no single definition of culture is universally embraced, one from the cultural anthropology perspective is "…a system of shared beliefs, values, customs, behaviors and artifacts that members of society use to cope with their worlds and with one another, and that are transmitted from generation to generation through learning." (Bates and Fratkin, 2002) Cultural groups are based on a wide range of factors, including geographic location, occupation, religion, sexual orientation, income, etc. Individuals may follow the beliefs and values of more than one culture concurrently. For instance, recent immigrants often espouse values and beliefs from both their original and adopted countries. Traditionally, social systems like education and healthcare have approached cultural diversity by focusing on race/ethnicity and common beliefs about various racial/ethnic group customs. These are frequently generalizations (e.g., lumping Mexican, Cuban, and Puerto Rican cultures together and describing them as "Latino" culture). This type of practice can lead to oversimplified stereotypes, and therefore to unrealistic behavioral expectations. Service professionals need more detailed knowledge of cultural complexities and subtleties to effectively engage and interact with families.

<u>Cultural paradigms of collectivism and individualism</u>
Certain world cultures are oriented more toward collectivism, while others are oriented more toward individualism. Native American, Latin American, Asian, and African cultures are more often collectivistic, focusing on interdependence, social interactions, relationships, and connections among individuals. North American, Canadian, European, and Australian cultures are more commonly individualistic, focusing on independence, uniqueness, self-determination, and self-actualization (realizing one's full potential). Individualism favors competition and distinguishing oneself as an individual, while collectivism favors cooperation that promotes and contributes to the harmony and well-being of the group. Individualist cultures value teaching young children object manipulation and scientific thinking, while collectivist cultures value social and relational behaviors. For example, adults in collectivist cultures may interpret a child's first steps as walking toward the adult, while adults in individualist cultures interpret them as developing motor skills and autonomy. These interpretations signify what each culture values most, forming the child's cultural orientation early in life. The planning and design of educational and other programs should be informed by a knowledge of these and other cultural differences.

Acculturation and assimilation

Acculturation describes the process whereby people adapt or change their cultural traditions, values, and beliefs as a result of coming into contact with and being influenced by other cultures over time. Some cultures adopt certain characteristics from other cultures they are exposed to, and two or more separate cultures may sometimes virtually fuse. However, assimilation, wherein various ethnic groups unite to form a new culture, is different from acculturation. One dominant culture may assimilate others. A historical example is the Roman Empire, which forced many members of ancient Greek, Hebrew, and other cultures to abandon their own cultures and adopt Roman law, military allegiance, traditions, language, religion, practices, and customs (including dress). The extent of a diverse cultural group's acculturation influences how it interacts with social systems like education and healthcare. Groups that are strongly motivated to maintain their cultural identity may interact less with mainstream systems that significantly conflict with or vary from their own cultural beliefs.

Measuring the acculturation

Social scientists currently use indices such as people's country of birth, how long they have lived in America, their knowledge of the English language, and their level of English language use to study acculturation. However, these factors are measured not because they are the core elements of acculturation, but because they are easier to validly and reliably measure than the underlying cultural beliefs, attitudes, and behaviors they reflect, which are harder to quantify. The interactions between American educators and culturally diverse families can be problematic on both sides. Educators have difficulty interacting, communicating, and collaborating with families that come from a variety of other countries, speak various other languages, and differ in their degree of acculturation to American culture. On the other hand, immigrant and culturally diverse families encounter a foreign language, different cultural customs and practices, and an unfamiliar educational system with different methods of assessment, placement, curriculum planning and design, instruction, and evaluation—not to mention different special education laws and procedures. Thus, the acculturation challenges related to interactions between American educators and culturally diverse families are bilateral.

Aspects of cultural competence at the system level within service systems

It is important for educational professionals to acquire and demonstrate cultural competence at the individual level to effectively interact with individual children and their families. Moreover, cultural competence is also important at the program level, the school level, and the system level. According to the National Center for Cultural Competence (NCCC), system level cultural competence is a continuing process that includes "...valuing diversity, conducting self-assessments (including organizational assessments), managing the dynamics of differences, acquiring and institutionalizing cultural knowledge, and adapting to the diversity and cultural contexts of the individuals and communities served." (Goode, 2001) Individual educational interactions are informed by a knowledge of cultural diversity and of the importance of such diversity in educational settings, an ability to adapt to the population's cultural needs, and a willingness to engage in ongoing self-reflection. This same set of knowledge and skills is also applied at the system level. Family engagement is important in EC care and education. This includes understanding the developmental needs of families as well as their children, especially when families and/or children speak different languages.

Culturally competent professional

A culturally competent professional demonstrates the ability to enable "...mutually rewarding interactions and meaningful relationships in the delivery of effective services for children and family whose cultural heritage differs from his or her own." (Shonkoff, National Research Council and Institute of Medicine, 2000) Providing interpreters and/or translators does not on its own constitute cultural competence. Hiring racially diverse educational staff in schools is also not enough. Culturally competent educators demonstrate highly developed self-awareness of their own cultural values and beliefs. They must also have and/or develop communication skills that allow them to elicit information from students and families regarding their own cultural beliefs. Further, they must be able to understand how diverse cultural views may affect a child's education, as well as how parents/families receive, comprehend, interpret, and respond to educators' communications. Therefore, educators must develop communication skills to meet educational goals.

Cultural differences in parents' goals for raising their children

Depending on their cultural group, parents have varying goals for their children, and use different practices to achieve those goals. For example, research on four different cultural groups in Hawaii found the following differences related to what parents visualized when they pictured their children as successful adults: Native Hawaiians most wanted their children to have social connections, be happy in their social networks, and demonstrate self-reliance as adults. Caucasian American parents most valued self-reliance, happiness, spontaneity, and creativity as developmental outcomes for their children. Filipino American parents most valued the development of traits related to obedience, citizenship, respect for authority, and good conduct and manners in their children. Japanese American parents placed priority on their children's achievement, as well as their ability to live well-organized lives, stay in contact with family, and master the demands of life. Such distinct, significant differences imply that these parent groups would vary in how they would respond to young children's assertive behaviors, in their disciplinary styles (e.g., permissive, authoritative, authoritarian), and in the emphasis they would place on activities focusing on physical and cognitive skill mastery vs. social competence and connection.

Differences in American parents

Parents in America have been found to show distinct preferences for the kinds of care and educational services they access for their children. For example, Caucasian parents in America are more likely to turn to preschool centers for help with their young children's care and instruction. This preference is influenced not only by custom, but also by scientific evidence that center-based preschool experience improves children's skills and prepares them for school. Hispanic parents in America are more likely to use home-based and/or family-based care settings. This preference probably reflects the more collectivist Hispanic perspective, which places more importance on social relationships than on structured learning in early childhood. Educators can take a culturally competent approach to such cultural diversity by looking for ways in which young children's school readiness skills can be promoted in family and home-based child care settings.

Depending on their native culture, parents vary in terms of the early experiences they select for their young children. For example, Latino parents tend to prefer family-based/home-based care. White parents tend to prefer center-based daycare and education designed to promote school readiness. Another cultural difference is parental beliefs about children's learning capacities. For example, research in California found that the majority of Latino parents believed their children's learning capacity is set at birth; only a small minority of white parents held this belief. Parents subscribing to a transactional child development model view the complex interaction between child and environment as creating a dynamic developmental process. These parents are more likely to value the stimulation of early childhood development, seek/implement activities that will provide such stimulation, and access early intervention services for children with developmental delays/difficulties. Parents subscribing to a view of fixed, innate cognitive capacity are less likely to believe their children's cognitive abilities can be influenced by educational experiences, and may not see the benefits of or seek out early learning stimulation and intervention.

Variations in reading to young children

Researchers analyzing national early childhood surveys have identified significant variations in how often white, Asian, and Hispanic parents read to their young children. This variation is not solely due to varying cultural values. Additional factors include parents' financial limitations; time limitations; familiarity and comfort with accessing libraries and other government resources, websites, etc.; and literacy levels in both English and their native languages. Educators must realize that trying to encourage or even teach parents to read to their children earlier and/or more often is unlikely to be successful if parents do not place value or priority on the benefits of being read to, or do not view the outcomes of reading aloud to children as benefits. Reading to children is known to promote school readiness and academic success. Educators should also understand that some parents, despite not being read to in early childhood, still become successful adults. Additionally, some cultures emphasize oral learning traditions more than written ones (e.g., many African American families engage in storytelling and singing more often than reading).

Developmental milestones and their associated ages that vary according to culture

Research has found that different cultures have different age expectations for many early childhood developmental milestones. For example, Filipinos expect children to eat using utensils at 32.4 months. Anglo families expect children to do this at 17.7 months, and Puerto Ricans expect children to reach this milestone at 26.5 months. Filipino cultures expect children to sleep all night by 32.4 months; Puerto Rican and Anglo cultures expect this at 14.5 and 14.4 months, respectively. Similarly, while Anglos expect children to sleep by themselves at around 13.8 months and Puerto Ricans at around 14.6 months, Filipinos do not expect this until 38.8 months. Filipinos expect children to eat solid food by 6.7 months; Anglos by 8.2 months; and Puerto Ricans by 10.1 months. In Anglo families, an 18-month-old not drinking from a cup could indicate developmental delay if parents introduced the cup when s/he was one year old and regularly continued encouraging cup use. But, Filipino parents of an 18-month-old have likely not even introduced the child to a cup yet, so the fact that the child is not using a cup would not be cause for concern from a development standpoint.

<u>Early milestones that have varying age expectations among different cultural groups</u>
When EC researchers investigated the average expectations of different cultural groups of when children would reach various developmental milestones, some of the milestones they examined included: eating solid food, weaning from nursing, drinking from a cup, eating with the fingers, eating with utensils, sleeping alone, sleeping through the night, choosing one's own clothes, dressing oneself, and playing alone. They also looked at daytime and nighttime toilet training. Educators must become aware of different cultures' different socialization goals before assuming culturally diverse children have developmental delays. On the other hand, they must also avoid automatically attributing variations in milestone achievement to cultural child rearing differences when full developmental assessments might be indicated. Family expectations and values influence the complex process of developmental assessment. When families and assessors share common cultures, it is more likely that valid data will be collected and interpreted. When their cultures differ, however, it is more likely that the assessment information will be misinterpreted. Employing EC teachers/care providers who are familiar with the child, family, and assessment setting as mediators can make developmental assessments more culturally competent.

Factors affecting parents who are immigrants to America

Parents educated in other countries may not know a great deal about the American educational system, and may not be aware of the educational demands made on their children, even in early childhood. Educators need to work with these parents to find common ground by identifying shared goals for children. While culturally diverse parents may disagree with some educators' goals, they can collaborate with educators to promote those on which they do agree. Immigrant parents may also be unaware of additional services available in America for children with developmental and/or learning problems. Educators can help parents by providing this information. Another consideration is that some other cultures have more paternalistic educational systems. Parents from such cultures, rather than vocally advocating for their children who need services, tend to wait for teachers/specialists to voice concerns before communicating any problems they have observed. Thus, they could miss out on the chance to obtain helpful services. Even worse, educators could misconstrue their behavior as a lack of interest in children's progress, or as resistance to confronting problems.

Essential concepts in geography

Ten concepts considered essential to the study of geography are: location, distance, achievability, pattern, morphology, agglomeration, utility value, interaction, area differentiation, and spatial interrelatedness. (1) Location: This concept identifies "where" a place is and examines the positive and negative properties of any place on the surface of the Earth. Absolute location is based upon latitude and longitude. Relative location is based upon changing characteristics of a region, and is influenced by surrounding areas. For example, urban areas have higher land prices than rural ones. (2) Distance: This identifies "how far" a place is, and is often described in terms of location. It is also related to the effort required to meet basic life needs. For example, the distance of raw materials from factories affects transportation costs and hence product prices. In another example, land costs less the farther it is from highways. (3) Achievability: The conditions on the Earth's surface dictate how accessible a geographic area is. For example, villages on beaches are easier to reach. Villages surrounded by forests or swamps are harder to reach. As its economy, science, technology, and transportation develop, a region's level of dependency on other areas changes.

Ten concepts considered essential to the study of geography are: location, distance, achievability, pattern, morphology, agglomeration, utility value, interaction, area differentiation, and spatial interrelatedness. (4) Patterns These are found in geographical forms and in how geographical phenomena spread, which affect dependency on those phenomena. For example, in fold regions (areas where the folding of rocks forms mountains), the rivers typically form trellis patterns. Patterns are also seen in human activity that is based on geography. For example, in mountainous regions, settlements predominantly form spreading patterns. (5) Morphology This is the shape of our planet's surface resulting from inner and outer forces. For example, along the northern coast of Java, sugarcane plantations predominate on the lowlands. (6) Agglomeration This is defined as collecting into a mass, and refers to a geographic concentration of people, activities, and/or settlements within areas that are most profitable and relatively narrow in size. (7) Utility value This refers to the existence and relative usefulness of natural resources. For example, fishermen find more utility value in the ocean than farmers do, and naturalists perceive more utility value in forests than academics would.

Ten concepts considered essential to the study of geography are: location, distance, achievability, pattern, morphology, agglomeration, utility value, interaction, area differentiation, and spatial interrelatedness. (8) Interaction This is the reciprocal and interdependent relationship between two or more geographical areas, which can generate new geographical phenomena, configurations, and problems. For example, a rural village produces raw materials through activities like mining ores or growing and harvesting plant crops, while a city produces industrial goods. The village needs the city as a market for its raw materials, and may also need the city's industrial products. The city needs the village for its raw materials to use in industrial production. This interdependence causes interaction. (9) Area differentiation This informs the study of variations among regional geographical phenomena. For example, different plants are cultivated in highlands vs. lowlands due to their different altitudes and climates. Area differentiation also informs the study of regional variations in occupation (farming vs. fishing, etc.). (10) Spatial interrelatedness This shows the relationship between/among geographic and non-physical phenomena, like rural and urban areas. The example above of village-city interaction also applies here.

Graphs

Graphs display numerical information in pictorial forms, making it easier to view statistics quickly and draw conclusions about them. For example, it is easier to see patterns/trends like increases/decreases in quantities using visual graphs than columns of numbers. Line graphs, bar graphs, and pie charts are the most common types of graphs. Line graphs depict changes over time by plotting points for a quantity measured each day/week/month/year/decade/century etc. and connecting the points to make a line. For example, showing the population of a city/country each decade in a line graph reveals how the population has risen/fallen/both. Bar graphs compare quantities related to different times/places/people/things. Each quantity is depicted by a separate bar, and its height/length corresponds to a number. Bar graphs make it easy to see which amounts are largest/smallest within a group (e.g., which of several cities/countries has the largest population). Pie charts/circle graphs divide a circle/"pie" into segments/"slices" showing percentages/parts of a whole, which also facilitates making comparisons. For example, the city/country with the largest population is the largest segment on a pie chart or circle graph.

Grid on a geographical map
Maps show absolute geographic location (i.e. the precise "address" of any place on the planet) using a grid of lines. The lines running from east to west are called parallels or latitudes, and they correspond to how many degrees away from the equator a place is located. The lines running from north to south are called meridians or longitudes, and they correspond to how many degrees away from the prime meridian a place is located. To determine the absolute location of a place, we find the spot on the map where its latitude and longitude intersect. This intersection is the place's absolute location. For example, if we look at Mexico City on a map, we will find that its latitude is 19° north and its longitude is 99° west, which is expressed in cartography as 19° N, 99° W. Numbers of latitudes and longitudes like these are also referred to as coordinates.

Tools that cartographers supply on maps
On maps depicting local, national, and world geography, cartographers supply tools for navigating these maps. For example, the compass rose indicates the directions of north, south, east, and west. By looking at the compass, people can identify the locational relationships of places (e.g., in South America, Chile is west of Argentina). The scale of miles indicates how distances on a map correspond to actual geographical distances, enabling us to estimate real distances. For example, the scale might show that one inch is equal to 500 miles. By placing a piece of paper on the map, we can mark it to measure the distance between two cities (e.g., Washington, DC, in the USA and Ottawa in Canada) on the map, and then line the paper up with the scale of miles to estimate an actual distance of approximately 650 miles between the two cities. Map keys/legends identify what a map's symbols and colors represent.

Categories of features that can be displayed on maps
Maps can be drawn to show natural or man-made features. For example, some maps depict mountains, elevations (altitudes), average rainfall, average temperatures, and other natural features of an area. Other maps are made to depict countries, states, cities, roads, empires, wars, and other man-made features. Some maps include both natural and man-made features (e.g., a map showing a certain country and its elevations). Different types of maps are described according to their purposes. For example, political maps are made to depict countries, areas within a country, and/or cities. Physical maps are drawn to display natural features of the terrain

in an area, such as rivers, lakes, and mountains. Thematic maps are drawn to focus on a more specific theme or topic, such as the locations and names of battles during a war or the average amounts of rainfall a country, state, or region receives in a given year or month. Some maps are made for more than one purpose, and indicate more than one of the types of information described above.

Reading and analyzing the information on a special purpose map
(1) First, read a map's title and look at the overall map. This provides a general idea of what the map shows. For example, a map entitled "Battles of the Punic Wars" would not be a good choice if someone was looking for the political boundaries of modern day Greece, Italy, and Spain. (2) Next, read the map's legend/key to see what symbols and colors the map uses, and what each represents. For example, some lines represent divisions between countries/states; some, roads; some, rivers; etc. Different colors can indicate different countries/states, elevations, amounts of rainfall, population densities, etc. These are not uniform across all maps, so legends/keys are necessary references. (3) Use the legend/key to interpret what the map shows. For example, by looking at colors representing elevations, one can determine which area of a country has the highest/lowest altitude. (4) Draw conclusions about what the map displays. For example, if a country map mainly has one color that indicates a certain elevation range, it can be concluded that this is the country's most common elevation.

Chronological thinking and understanding history

To see cause-and-effect relationships in historical events and explore and understand relationships among those events, students must have a solid grasp of when things happened and in what time sequence (chronology). Teachers can help students develop chronological thinking by using and assigning well-constructed/well-written narratives. These include histories written in the same style as stories, works of historical literature, and biographies. These hold students' attention, allowing them to focus on authors' depictions of temporal relationships among antecedents, actions, and consequences; of historical motivations and deeds of individuals and groups; and of the time structure of sequential occurrences. By middle school, students should have the skills needed to measure time mathematically (e.g., in years/decades/centuries/millennia), interpret data displayed in timelines, and calculate time in BCE and CE. High school students should be able to analyze patterns of historical duration (e.g., how long the U.S. Constitutional government has lasted) and patterns of historical succession (e.g., the development of expanding trade and communication systems, from Neolithic times through ancient empires and from early modern times to modern global interaction).

Students should be able to differentiate among past, present, and future. They should be able to identify the beginning, middle, and end/outcome of historical narratives/stories. They also should be able to construct their own historical narratives, including working forward and backward in time from some event to explain causes and temporal development of various events, issues, etc. Students should be able to calculate and measure calendar time, including days/dates, weeks, months, years, centuries, and millennia. They should be able to describe time periods using BCE/BC and CE/AD. They should be skilled at comparing calendar systems (e.g., Roman, Gregorian, Julian, Hebrew, Muslim, Mayan, and others) and at relating the calendar years of major historical events. They should be able to look at timelines and interpret the information they contain, and make their own timelines using equidistant time intervals and recording events sequentially. Students should be able to explain change and continuity in history through reconstructing and applying patterns of historical duration and succession. They should be able to identify the structural principles that are the bases of alternative periodization models, and to compare these models.

Our country's laws and rules

Young children must understand the purposes of rules/laws: They identify acceptable/unacceptable citizen behaviors; make society and life predictable, secure, and orderly; designate responsibilities to citizens; and prevent persons in authority positions from abusing their roles by limiting their power. Understanding these functions of laws/rules enables children to realize that our government consists of individuals and groups authorized to create, implement, and enforce laws and manage legal disputes. Some creative EC teachers have used children's literature to illustrate these concepts. Children can relate personally to stories' characters, and story situations make the concepts real and concrete to children. Stories can be springboards for discussing rules and when they do/do not apply. One activity involves children in small groups making class rules (e.g., "No talking" and "Stay in your seat"), and then rewriting these to be more realistic (e.g., "Talk softly in class; listen when others talk" and "Sit down and get right to work"). Children consider issues of safety and fairness, and develop an understanding of judicial and legislative roles.

Mathematics

Problem solving skills

Being able to solve problems is fundamental to all other components of mathematics. Children learn the concept that a question can have more than one answer and a problem can have more than one solution by participating in problem solving activities. To solve problems, a child must be able to explore a problem, a situation, or a subject; think through the problem, situation, or subject; and use logical reasoning. These abilities are needed to not only solve routine/everyday problems, but also novel/unusual ones. Using problem solving skills not only helps children think mathematically, but also promotes their language development and their social skills when they work together. Children are naturally curious about how to solve everyday problems. Adults can take advantage of this inherent curiosity by discussing everyday challenges, asking children to propose ways to solve them, and asking them to explain how they arrived at their solutions. Adults can also invite children to propose problems and ask questions about them. This helps them learn to analyze different types of problems and realize that many problems have multiple possible solutions.

Steps preparing young children to learn
The process of solving problems often involves the following steps: understanding the problem; coming up with a plan to solve the problem; putting that plan into action; and, finally, observing the outcome and reflecting on whether the solution was effective, and whether the answer arrived at makes sense. Solving problems not only involves learning this series of steps, but also requires children to develop the qualities needed to solve problems. Children who are able to solve problems have a number of characteristics. For example, children who are effective problem solvers are able to focus their attention on the problem and its individual component parts. They can formulate hypotheses about the problem/situation, and then test them for veracity. They are willing to take risks within reason. They are persistent if they do not solve a problem right away, and do not give up if their first attempt at solving a problem is unsuccessful. They maintain flexibility, and experiment with alternate methods. They also demonstrate self-regulation skills.

Using problem solving skills in daily life
Young children continually explore their environments to unravel mysteries about how things work. For example, preschoolers use math concepts to understand that they have three toys, to comprehend that three fingers equals three toys, or to understand that two cookies plus one more equals three cookies. To do abstract mathematics in the future, young children will need two major skills that are also used to solve problems: being able to visualize a scenario, and being able to apply common sense thinking. Thinking and planning to achieve goals within the constraints of the properties of the surrounding environment is a natural behavior for young children. They will persist in their efforts to get an older sibling to stop another activity to play with them, to repair broken toys with tape or chewing gum, to manipulate a puzzle or plastic building blocks to get one uncooperative piece to fit, etc. The great 20th century mathematician and teacher George Polya stated that problem solving is "the most characteristically human activity." He pointed out that problem solving is a skill learned by doing, and that developing this skill requires a great deal of practice.

Games/activities
One method that has been found to enhance children's reasoning skills is using adult-child conversations to play mental mathematics games. For example, once children are able to count beyond five, adults can give them basic oral story problems to solve (e.g., "If you have two plums and I give you two more, how many will you have?"). Using children's favorite foods in story problems, which takes advantage of their ready ability to envision these foods, is a good place to start. Thereafter, adults can add story problems involving pets, toys, cars, shopping, and other familiar objects/animals/activities. Experts advise adults not to restrict the types of problems presented to a child based solely on the child's grade level. Children can work with any situation if

they can form mental imagery. Adults can sometimes insert harder tasks (e.g., problems involving larger numbers, problems involving division with remainders, or problems with negative number answers). Even toddlers can solve problems such as how to divide three cookies between two people. The division may not be fair, but it will likely be efficient. Adults should use the Socratic method, asking guiding questions to allow children to arrive at a solution to a problem themselves, rather than telling them a "right" answer.

Mental math games

Adults can use children's favorite foods and toys to pose story problems to children that involve addition and subtraction. For example, they can ask them questions like "If I give you [this many] more, how many will you have?" or "If we take away [this many], how many are left?" It is better to ask children questions than to give them answers. It is important to use turn taking. In this method, the adult poses a story problem to the child, and then the child gets to pose one to the adult. Adults must try to solve the problem, even if the child makes up numbers like "bazillion" or "eleventy." Games should be fun, not strictly factual like math tests. Adults can introduce age-appropriate story topics as children grow older. At the end of early childhood/around school age, children can handle the abstract algebraic concept of variables/unknown numbers (which some experts call "mystery numbers") and use this concept in games. Adults can pose riddles where "x" or "n" is the unknown number, and children must use an operation (e.g., $x + 4 = 7$) to solve the riddle.

Communicating with children to promote mathematical reasoning skills

Adults reciprocally talk to and listen to children during communication that is focused on using mathematical skills like problem solving, reasoning, making connections, etc. To promote young children's understanding, adults can express mathematical concepts using pictures, words, diagrams, and symbols. Encouraging children to talk with their peers and adults helps them clarify their own thoughts and think about what they are doing. Communicating with children about mathematical thinking problems also develops their vocabularies and promotes early literacy and reading skills. Adults should listen to what children want to say, and should have conversations with them. Communicating about math can also be accomplished through reading children's books that incorporate numbers and/or repetition or rhyme. In addition to talking, adults can communicate math concepts to children by drawing pictures or diagrams and using concrete objects (e.g., blocks, crayons, pieces of paper, fingers, etc.) to represent numbers and/or solve problems. Children also share their learning of math concepts through words, charts, drawings, tallies, etc. Even toddlers hold up fingers to tell others how old they are.

Reasoning skills appling early mathematical and scientific concepts

A major component of problem solving is reasoning. Children reason when they think through questions and find usable answers. They use reasoning skills to make sense of mathematical and scientific subject matter. Children use several abilities during the reasoning process. For example, they use logic to classify objects or concepts into groups. They follow logical sequences to arrive at conclusions that make sense. They use their analytical abilities to explain their own thought processes. They apply what they have learned about relationships and patterns to help them find solutions to problems. They also use reasoning to justify their mental processes and problem solutions. To support children's reasoning, adults can ask children questions, give them time to think about their answers, and listen to their answers. This simple tactic helps children learn how to reason. Adults can also ask children why something is as it is—letting them think for themselves rather than looking for a particular answer—and listen to the ideas they produce.

Making connections in children's early mathematical development

Children informally learn intuitive mathematical thinking through their everyday life experiences. They naturally apply mathematical concepts and reasoning to solve problems they face in their environment. However, one frequent problem among children when they begin formal education is that they can come to see academic mathematics as a collection of procedures and rules, instead of viewing it as a means of finding solutions to everyday, real-life problems. This view will interfere with children's ability to apply the formal mathematics they learn to their lives in a practical and useful way. Teachers can help prevent this outcome by establishing the connection between children's natural intuitive math and formal mathematics. They can do this by teaching math through the use of manipulative materials familiar to children. They can use mathematics vocabulary words when describing children's activities, which enables children to develop an awareness of the natural mathematical operations they use in their daily lives. When a teacher introduces a new mathematical concept to children, s/he can give illustrative examples that draw upon the children's actual life experiences.

Mathematics and everyday life and other academic subjects

We use math throughout our lives during everyday activities. There are countless examples and combinations of various mathematical concepts in the real world. Additionally, math concepts inform other academic content areas, including music, art, and the sciences. Therefore, it is important for children not to view math as an isolated set of procedures and skills. Children comprehend math more easily when they can make connections, which involve applying common mathematical rules to multiple, varied functions, processes, and real-life activities. For example, adults can ask children to consider problems they encounter daily and solve them. When a parent asks a child to help put away groceries, the child practices sorting categories of foods and packages, and experiments with comparative package sizes and shapes. Parents need not be concerned with what specific mathematical processes are involved, but should simply look for examples of math in everyday life and expose children to these examples on a regular basis. For example, pouring liquid into containers of various sizes and speculating which one will hold the most is an easy, fun activity that incorporates a number of skills and concepts, including estimation, measurement, spatial sense, and conservation of liquid volume.

<u>Integrating math into everyday activities</u>
Integrating math into the context of everyday activities has been the philosophy of early childhood math education until recently. For example, when teachers have children line up, they ask them who is first, second, third, etc. to practice counting. When children play with blocks, teachers ask them to identify their shapes and whether one block is larger/smaller than another. During snack times, teachers help children learn 1:1 correspondence by having them place one snack on each plate. These activities are quite valuable. However, some educators maintain that they are insufficient when used on their own, because in larger classes it is not always possible to take advantage of "teachable moments" with every child. Therefore, this educational approach cannot be applied systematically. These educators recommend that in addition to integration strategies, EC teachers should use a curriculum. The HighScope curriculum, the Creative Curriculum, and Big Math for Little Kids are just a few examples. Many teachers combine several curricula, selecting parts of different programs. Using a curriculum allows teachers to use a more planned approach to integrate math into all activities.

Representation skills

Young children develop an understanding of symbolic representation—the idea that objects, written letters, words, and other symbols are used to represent other objects or concepts—at an early age. This is evident in their make-believe/pretend play, and in their ability to learn written language and connect it to spoken language. As children develop early math skills, representing their ideas and information they acquire helps them organize, document, and share these ideas and facts with others. Children may count on their fingers; create tallies using check marks/tick marks and/or words; draw pictures or maps; and, as they grow older, make graphs. Teachers must help children apply mathematical process skills as they use learning center materials. For example, when a child enjoys sorting rocks by color, the teacher can state that the child is classifying them, bridging informal math activities with math vocabulary. Asking the child how s/he is categorizing the rocks emphasizes math vocabulary. Asking the child after s/he finishes what other ways s/he could classify the rocks encourages problem solving.

Patterns and relationships

Patterns are generally defined as things that recur or are repeated regularly. Patterns can be found in images, sounds, numbers, events, actions, movements, etc. Relationships are generally defined as connections or associations between things that are identified and/or described using logic or reasoning. Being aware of patterns and relationships among aspects of the environment helps us comprehend the fundamental structure of these aspects. This awareness enables us to predict what will occur next in a series of events, even before it actually happens. This gives us more confidence in our environment and in our ability to interact with it. We find patterns and relationships in such areas of life as art, music, and clothing. Math-specific activities like counting numbers and working with geometrical shapes, lines, arcs, and curves also involve patterns and relationships. When children understand patterns and relationships, they can understand repetition; rhythm; categorization; and how to order things from smallest to biggest, from shortest to longest, etc.

Adults can help young children develop their understanding of patterns and relationships in life by looking at pictures and designs with them, encouraging and guiding them to identify patterns within drawings, paintings, and abstract designs such as prints on fabrics and other decorative designs. When children participate in movement activities, including dancing to music, running, skipping, hopping, playing simple musical instruments, etc., adults can help them identify patterns in their own and others' movements. Adults can encourage young children to participate in hands-on activities, such as stringing wood, plastic beads, or penne and other hollow dry pasta tubes onto pieces of string to make necklaces with simple patterns (e.g., blue-yellow-blue-yellow). As children grow older, adults can encourage them to create more complicated patterns. They can alternate a larger number of colors, and they can vary the numbers of each color in more complex ways (e.g., three blue, two yellow, one red, etc.).

Number sense and number operations

Counting is one of the earliest numeracy skills that young children develop. Even before they have learned the names of all the numbers, young children learn to count to three, then to five, etc. However, number sense involves a great deal more than just counting. Number sense includes understanding the various applications of numbers. For instance, we use numbers as tools for conveying and manipulating information, as tools for describing quantities, and as tools for characterizing relationships between or among things. Children who have developed number sense are able to count with accuracy and competence. Given a specific number, they can count upwards from that number. They can also count backwards. They are able to break down a number and then reassemble it. They are able to recognize relationships between or among different numbers. When children can count, are familiar with numbers, and have good number sense, they can also add and subtract numbers. Being familiar with numbers and being able to count easily helps young children understand all other areas of mathematics.

Developing number sense and numeracy skills

As children complete their daily activities, it is beneficial for adults to count real things with children and encourage them to count as well. This helps children understand numbers by using their own experiences with objects in the environment, and gives them practice counting and using numbers. To help children understand that we use numbers to describe quantities and relationships, adults can ask children to sort objects by size, shape, or color similarity. They can also ask children to sort objects according to their differences (e.g., which object is bigger/smaller). Adults can also discuss with children how numbers are used to find street addresses and apartment numbers, and to keep score during games. To help children count upwards and downwards with efficiency and accuracy, adults can point out that counting allows us to determine how many items are in a group. Adults should point to each object as they count it. They can count on their fingers and encourage young children to do the same. Adults should also help children count without repeating or skipping any numbers.

Spatial sense and geometry

Spatial sense is an individual's awareness of one's own body in space and in relation to the objects and other people around the individual. Spatial sense allows young children to navigate environmental spaces without colliding with objects and other people; to see and hear adequately, and to be aware of whether others can see and hear them; and to develop and observe a socially and culturally appropriate sense of their own and others' personal space. Geometry is the area of mathematics involving space, sizes, shapes, positions, movements, and directions. Geometry gives descriptions and classifications of our physical environment. By observing commonplace objects and spaces in their physical world, young children can learn about solid objects and substances, shapes, and angles. Adults can help young children learn geometry by identifying various shapes, angles, and three-dimensional figures for them; asking them to name these shapes, angles, and figures when they encounter them in the future; and asking them to describe different shapes, draw them in the air with their fingers, trace drawings of the shapes with their fingers, and then draw the shapes themselves.

Because it involves many physical properties like shape, line, and angle, as well as abstract concepts, young children learn geometry most effectively via hands-on activities. Learning experiences that allow them to touch and manipulate concrete objects, such as boxes, containers, puzzles, blocks, and shape sorters, usually work best. Everyday activities can also help children learn geometry concepts. For example, adults can cut children's sandwiches into various geometrical shapes and let children fit them together and/or rearrange them into new patterns. Children become better able to follow directions and navigate through space when they develop geometric knowledge and spatial sense. Adults can provide activities that promote the development of geometric knowledge and spatial sense. For example, they can let children get into and out of big appliance boxes; climb over furniture; and go into, on top of, out of, under, around, over, and through different objects and structures to allow children to experience the relationship between their bodies and space and solids. As they mature, children can play games in which they search for "hidden" shapes. Such shapes may be irregular, may lack flat bases, or may be turned in various directions.

Measurement

Measurement is the process of determining how long, wide, and tall something is physically and how much it weighs by using measuring units such as inches, feet, yards, square feet, ounces, and pounds. Measurement is also used to quantify time using units like seconds, minutes, hours, days, weeks, months, years, centuries, millennia, etc. Measurement is not just a formal means of quantifying size, area, and time. It is also an important method for young children to seek and identify relationships between and among things they encounter outside of school in everyday life. When young children practice measuring things, they are able to understand not only the sizes of objects and beings, but also their comparative sizes (i.e. how large or small something is compared to another object used as a reference). Furthermore, they are able to figure out how big or little something is on their own.

While it is obviously important for children to eventually learn standardized measurement units like inches, feet, yards, etc., adults can facilitate early development of measurement skills by letting children choose their own measurement units. For example, they might use their favorite toy to describe a playmate or sibling as "three teddy bears tall"; or they might describe a room as "seven toy cars long." Similarly, when children are too young to know formal time measurements like minutes and hours, adults can support children's ability to quantify time using favorite TV shows. For example, four-year-olds can often relate to the idea of one episode of a show (whether it is 30 minutes or 60 minutes long) as a time measurement. Adults can apply this with statements like, "Daddy will be home in one episode." Numerous everyday activities, including grocery shopping, cooking, sewing, gardening, woodworking, and many others, involve measurement. Adults can ask children to help with these tasks, and then discuss measuring with children as they participate.

Measurement of time

Younger children typically do not have an understanding of the abstract concept of time. However, adults can still help children understand that time elapses, and that we count/measure this process. For example, adults can ask younger children simple questions, such as "Who can stand on one foot longer?" This comparison strategy helps children figure out which of two or more actions/activities takes a longer/the longest period of time. Even when children do not yet understand what "five minutes" means, adults should still make such references (e.g., "You can play for five minutes longer, and then we must leave."). Repeating such references will eventually help children understand that time passes. Adults can time various everyday activities/events and tell children how long they took. They can also count the second hand's ticks on a watch/clock (e.g., "one second...two seconds...three seconds..."). This familiarizes children with counting, and with using counting to track the passage of time. Until children are old enough to understand abstractions like today/yesterday/tomorrow, adults can use concrete references like "after lunch" or "before bedtime."

Fractions

Fractions are parts or pieces of a whole. While adults understand this and do not remember ever not understanding it, very young children think differently in this regard. As Piaget showed, children in the preoperational stage of cognitive development cannot perform logical or mathematical mental operations. They focus on one property of an object rather than all of its properties, a practice he called centration. Hence, if you cut an apple into pieces, very young children see that there are more pieces than there were before, and they believe that several apple pieces are more than one apple. They cannot yet comprehend the logical sequence of dividing an apple into fractions. To comprehend fractions, children must know what a whole unit consists of, how many pieces the unit is divided into, and whether the pieces are of equal size. Adults can help children understand fractions through informal sharing activities, such as slicing up a pizza or a pan of brownies, and/or equally dividing household/preschool chores and play materials.

Estimation

Estimation is making an educated or informed guess about a measurement when no actual measurement is available. As adults, we often make estimates about the sizes of objects when we do not know their exact measurements, about the amounts of substances we have not actually measured, and about the numbers of small objects in large collections when we have not actually counted the objects. However, young children are in the process of learning the concepts of sizes and numbers. Children must comprehend concepts of comparison and relativity (e.g., larger, smaller, more, less, etc.) before they will be able to make accurate estimates. When children start to develop the ability to estimate amounts or sizes, this process helps them learn related math vocabulary words, such as "about" or "around," and "more than" and "less than" [something else]. Through estimating, they also learn how to make appropriate predictions and arrive at realistic answers. It is important for young children to learn how to make estimates, to recognize when it is appropriate to apply the estimation method, and to recognize when their estimates are reasonable.

To accustom young children to the idea of estimating, adults should regularly use words related to estimation in their conversations with children (e.g., "around," "about," "approximately," "near," "more than [some other amount or number]," "less than [some other amount or number]," "between [two numbers or amounts]," etc.). During everyday activities like shopping or eating, adults can ask children to estimate amounts of foods, numbers of items, or lengths of time. Later, adults can help children compare the actual outcome with their original estimate. This process helps children learn to make realistic/reasonable estimates. Activities promoting estimation skills can be very simple. Adults can ask children, for example, to guess which of their friends is tallest, and then test the accuracy of the guess using real measurements. When children grow older, adults can write down estimates and real measurements, and can then repeat the exercise described above or present a similar one. With repetition, children will eventually begin making more accurate estimates. The goal is not for children to come up with exact measurements, but ones that are close to actual amounts/numbers. Giving children opportunities to practice improves their estimating skills.

Probabilities and statistics

In general, when people work with statistics, they present them in graphs or charts to organize them, interpret them, and make it easier to see relationships among individual statistics. Graphs are a visual alternative that depict mathematical information and show relationships among individual statistics, especially changes over time. Graphs also allow for the comparison of different groups. Probabilities indicate the likelihood that something will happen. Adults use probabilities to predict things, such as people's risks of developing or dying from various diseases or medical conditions; the chances of accidents; children's risks of experiencing academic difficulties, dropping out, or developing emotional and behavioral disorders; and the chances that a certain area will receive rain or snow. Scientists use probabilities to predict the likelihood of various behaviors or outcomes they are studying. They use statistics to show the numbers and proportions of responses or results obtained in research studies. Calendars are one type of chart. Adults can help children use them to organize daily and weekly activities, and to understand how we organize information.

Charts and graphs

According to experts, almost every daily activity can be charted in some way. For example, adults can help children peel the little stickers off of plums, bananas, etc. and stick them to a piece of paper/poster board divided into columns. After a week, they can count each column to determine how many pieces of each kind of fruit they ate. Similarly, adults can show children how to use removable stickers or color forms to document the number of times they performed any daily activity. For example, children could place a color form near the telephone every time it rings and/or every time somebody picks it up to make a call. They could also place a color form near the front door every time somebody comes in, goes out, and/or rings the doorbell/knocks. This enables children to count the number of times given events occur by recording them. Some children are better able to understand math by viewing and making graphs. This is because creating graphs involves representing quantities visually instead of just listing numbers.

Mathematical milestones

Counting is considered a math skill milestone for young children. Typical four-year-olds enjoy counting aloud. Experts identify three levels of counting. The first is counting from 1 to 12, which requires memorization. The second level is counting from 13 to 19, which requires not only memorization, but also an understanding of the more unusual rules for "teen" numbers. The third level is counting from 20 on. This process is very consistent, and the numbers are ordered according to regular rules. Experts in math education believe that at this level of counting, children are discovering a regular mathematical pattern for the first time, which is base ten (i.e. 20, 30, 40, 50, etc. are 2 tens, 3 tens, 4 tens, 5 tens, etc., and after the base a number between 1 and 9 is added). Researchers and educators in early childhood mathematics programs recommend encouraging children as young as four years old to learn to count up to 100. They find that doing this helps young children learn about and explore patterns in depth.

Clinical interview

Clinical interviews have long been used by individual and family therapists, as well as by researchers. Piaget used them along with observations and case histories to understand young children's thinking as he formulated his cognitive developmental theory. Interviewers ask structured/semi-structured/open-ended questions and listen to the responses, often recording them for accuracy. This method gives the interviewer a way to find out what the respondent is thinking and feeling inside, which cannot be determined by observing outward behaviors alone. In educational settings, a teacher might ask a child questions like, "How did you do this?" "What is happening now?" "Can you tell me more about this?" "Why are you doing this?" "What are you thinking about now?" etc. Flexible questioning helps uncover the child's thought process, which is what is leading him/her to engage in specific behaviors. Just observing the behaviors alone does not allow the child to express his/her knowledge. While fully interviewing each child in a classroom is not practical, teachers can adapt this method by asking clinical interview-type questions as part of their instruction.

Teachers can gain a lot of information and insight about how children are learning math concepts by observing their behaviors. For children to actually express their knowledge and thinking processes, however, teachers must ask them questions. For example, when a teacher introduces new shapes to young children, s/he can ask them the shapes' names, how they differ from one another, and why they think the shapes differ. Teachers can then use children's various responses to elicit further responses from them. This technique requires children to use language in significant ways during math activities. Therefore, these activities not only teach math skills, but also promote literacy development. Asking clinical interview-type questions promotes children's development of math communication skills, one of the essential components of math education. Additionally, being able to put one's knowledge and thoughts into words is a skill that is very important in all areas of education, not just math education. Using clinical interview-type questions helps children learn to use language to explain their thinking, share ideas, and express themselves, promoting and strengthening children's awareness of the functions of mathematical language.

Young children's thinking and learning

Young children think in concrete ways and cannot understand abstract concepts, so effective EC math curricula typically use many concrete objects that children can see, feel, and manipulate to help them understand math concepts. Young children also naturally learn through exploring their environments, so good EC math curricula have many exploration and discovery activities that allow and encourage hands-on learning. In everyday life, young children start to observe relationships as they explore their surroundings. They match like objects, sort unlike objects, categorize objects, and arrange objects in simple patterns based on shared or contrasting properties. They start to understand words and phrases like "a little," "a lot," "more," "less," and "the same [as...]." Preschoolers use available materials such as sticks, pieces of string, their feet, their hands, their fingers, etc. as tools to measure objects. They also use rulers, measuring cups, and other conventional tools. They use their measurements to develop descriptions, sequences, and arrangements, and to compare various objects.

Spatial awareness

When preschool children build structures with blocks and put together pieces of puzzles during play, they are not only having fun, but are also developing spatial awareness. The relationships of objects to each other and within space are important concepts for children to learn, and serve as a foundation for the principles of geometry and physics that children will learn later. When they are moving around, preschoolers begin to notice how other people and objects are positioned in space, and how their own bodies move through space in relationship to objects and other people. This type of spatial awareness supports children's developing gross motor skills, coordination, and social skills. Young children can and should learn a number of math concepts and skills, such as the ones recommended by preschool math curricula like the HighScope program's "Numbers Plus" preschool mathematics curriculum. These concepts and skills include number symbols and names, counting, shapes, spatial awareness, relationships of parts to the whole, measurement, units, patterns, and analyzing data.

Rational numbers and irrational numbers

In mathematics, rational numbers are numbers that can be written as ratios or fractions. In other words, a rational number can be expressed as a fraction that has a whole number as the numerator (the number on top) and the denominator (the number on the bottom). Therefore, all whole numbers are automatically rational numbers, because all whole numbers can be written as fractions with a denominator of 1 (e.g., 5 = 5/1, 68 = 68/1, 237 = 237/1, etc.). Even very large, unwieldy fractions (e.g., 9,731,245/42,754,021) are rational numbers, because they can be written as fractions. Irrational numbers can be written as decimal numbers, but not as fractions, because the numbers to the right of the decimal point that are less than 1 continue indefinitely without repeating. For example, the value of pi (π) begins as 3.141592..., and continues without end. The square root of 2 ($\sqrt{2}$) = 1.414213.... There are an infinite number of irrational numbers between 0 and 1. However, irrational numbers are not used as commonly in everyday life as rational numbers.

Cardinal, ordinal, nominal, and real numbers

Cardinal numbers are numbers that indicate quantity. For example, when we say "seven buttons" or "three kittens," we are using cardinal numbers. Ordinal numbers are numbers that indicate the order of items within a group or a set. For example, when we say "first, second, third, fourth, fifth, etc.," we are using ordinal numbers. Nominal numbers are numbers that name things. For example, we use area code numbers along with telephone numbers to identify geographical calling areas, and we use zip code numbers to identify geographical mailing areas. Nominal numbers, therefore, identify categories or serve as labels for things. However, they are not related to the actual mathematical values of numbers, and do not indicate numerical quantities or operations. Real numbers include all rational and irrational numbers. Rational numbers can always be written as fractions that have both numerators and denominators that are whole numbers. Irrational numbers cannot, as they contain non-repeating decimal digits. Real numbers may or may not be cardinal numbers.

Button board

By gluing buttons of various sizes and colors to a piece of cardboard, teachers can initiate a number of activities that help preschoolers learn math concepts while having fun. Preschoolers are commonly learning shapes and how to draw them. Teachers can give children lengths of string/twine/yarn or long shoelaces and show them how to wrap them around different buttons to form shapes like rectangles, triangles, and squares. To practice counting and 1:1 correspondence, teachers can ask children to wrap their string around a given number of buttons. Preschoolers need to learn the concept that spoken number words like "five" can equate to a group of five concrete objects (such as buttons), and this activity promotes that learning. The button board is also useful for giving preschool children practice with sorting or classifying objects into groups based on a common characteristic. For example, the teacher can ask children to wrap their pieces of string around all the big buttons, all the little buttons, only the red buttons, only the blue buttons, etc.

Making mathematics fun

Teachers can encourage preschool children's counting and number development by creating a grid on the floor with the numbers 1 to 10 using masking tape, construction paper, and markers. Teachers could also draw the grid outdoors by drawing on pavement with chalk. The teacher arranges the numbers in ascending order within the grid of 10 squares/rectangles. S/he asks the children if they can name these numbers. The teacher provides beanbags. Each child gets a chance to throw a beanbag into any one of the numbered squares. Children can see how far they can throw and/or practice their aim. Each child names the number inside the square/rectangle where his/her beanbag lands. The children then play a version of hopscotch by hopping from numbered square to square, collecting their beanbags, and then hopping back. If desired, the teacher can write the number each child's beanbag lands on onto a "scoreboard" graph. Children will observe his/her writing the same numbers found on the floor/ground onto a "scoreboard." Teachers can review learning after the game to assess whether children can count using number words, name selected numbers, and throw accurately with consistency.

<u>Reusing sectioned plastic trays from the grocery store</u>
A teacher can wash and reuse the compartmentalized plastic trays from the grocery store that are used for vegetable and fruit to create a preschool counting activity. The teacher supplies beads, pennies, erasers, or other small objects, as well as about a dozen sticky notes. S/he writes a number on each note. For older preschoolers, the teacher can write the numeral and the word (e.g., "7" and "seven"). For younger children, the teacher can write the numeric symbol ("7," for example) plus seven dots or other marks as a clue to that number symbol. The teacher puts one numbered note in each compartment and the supply of small objects in the central dip compartment. Then, s/he guides each child to transfer the correct number of each small object to the correct compartment. The child should count aloud while transferring each small object, and should repeat this process until all compartments with a numbered sticky note have the correct number of objects. Children can then repeat the process to practice and perfect their counting, or the teacher can place notes with different numbers in the tray's compartments.

<u>Game that teachers can create for the practicing of practice number recognition</u>
Teachers can help preschoolers practice identifying numbers and counting by creating a fun "fishing for numbers" game. Teachers cut 10 fish shapes that are about 6 inches long from pieces of construction paper that are different colors. Teachers then write a single number between 1 and 10 on each "fish." Near each fish "mouth," the teacher punches a hole and inserts a paper clip through it. The teacher makes "fishing rods" by tying strings to dowels and gluing a magnet to each string. After spreading out the fish so the children can easily see the numbers, the teacher assigns each child a number and they "fish" for it, picking up the fish by bringing the magnet close to the paper clip. The children then "reel in" their catches. This gives children practice correctly identifying number names. The game can be adapted for more advanced math concepts as well.

For example, the teacher can cut out fish shapes of various sizes and have children "fish" for larger/smaller fish. The activity can also be adapted to promote literacy development. The teacher can write letters instead of numbers on the fish to give students practice with alphabet recognition, or s/he can write a Dolch word/sight word on each fish to give students practice recognizing and identifying important vocabulary words.

Creating collages
Fundamental math skills that prepare preschoolers for kindergarten include shape recognition. To introduce children to an activity they will view as fun rather than as work, teachers can show children how to make a collage of a familiar figure. This will also give children the opportunity to experiment with an artistic process. For example, they can create a Santa Claus or an Easter Bunny as a holiday art project. They can make collages of other imaginary/real people for various events/seasons/topics. Teachers cut out paper templates, including circles for heads, triangles for hats, squares for bodies, and narrow rectangular strips for limbs. First, they help children name each shape. They have each child trace the template shapes onto paper and cut them out with child-safe scissors. The teacher then instructs children to arrange their cutout shapes on a piece of cardboard/construction paper. Once they are in the correct positions, the children glue the shapes in place. Teachers can subsequently teach additional shapes (octagons, ovals, etc.), challenging children to make new, different collages.

Red Rover game
Red Rover is a good game for groups of children who are attending parties or playing outdoors at parks/playgrounds. Two teams take turns calling and roving. The child called runs to the other team and tries to fit into its line. If successful, s/he gets to call another player to bring back to his/her home team. If not, s/he joins the opposite team. The game continues until one team has no more members. Teachers can adapt this game to teach shape recognition by cutting out various shapes from construction paper of different colors and pinning a shape to each child's shirt. In large groups, more than one child can have the same shape or color. Instead of children's names, the teacher instructs players to use shapes and colors when calling (e.g., "Red Rover, Red Rover, blue circles come over!"). This supports the development of shape and color recognition skills. Teachers can vary action verbs (e.g., "....hop over/jump over/skip over") to support vocabulary development and comprehensive skills. When children perform such movements, they are also practicing and developing gross motor skills.

Cookie baking activity
Young children are typically curious about adult activities like baking. They usually want to know more about the process, and often ask many questions. They also love to be included and to participate, frequently offering/asking to help. Letting them help builds their self-esteem and self-efficacy (i.e. their confidence in their competence to accomplish a task). Adults can allow children to help while also providing instruction and practice with shape recognition, measurement, sorting, and categorization. The adult prepares a favorite cookie recipe. Some children can help measure ingredients, which helps develop the math skill of measurement. With the dough rolled out, children use cookie cutters of various shapes. Recognizing, naming, and selecting the shapes promote the development of shape recognition skills. Adults "shuffle"/mix the baked cookie shapes and have children separate cookies with like shapes into groups, which promotes sorting skills. Having children identify similar/different shapes, sizes, and colors promotes categorization skills. Arranging cookie shapes into patterns for children to identify promotes pattern recognition skills, which are necessary to the development of math skills and many other skills. Giving each child a cookie to eat afterward is naturally reinforcing.

Pasta necklace making as a learning activity
Stringing beads/noodles is an activity that helps young children develop hand-eye coordination, which they will need for writing and other everyday activities that require fine motor coordination. Noodles are typically the perfect size for young children's hands. They are inexpensive, usually costing less than comparably-sized beads. Moreover, pasta is non-toxic, an advantage when working with little persons who put things in their mouths. Hollow, tubular noodles like penne, ziti,

wagon wheels, etc. are ideal. Fishing line/craft beading string/other stiff string is best; soft, limp string/yarn is harder for young children to manipulate. Using multicolored vegetable pasta removes the need to use markers or dye to add color. If using white pasta, children can color the noodles with markers, but adults should keep in mind that the ink can bleed onto skin/clothes even when it is dry. Adults should cut pieces of string that are long enough to allow children to easily slip the necklaces on and off after they are tied. Adults should also use a knot to secure a noodle to one end of the string. By providing more than one noodle shape, adults can invite children to string the noodles to create patterns, which develops pattern recognition and pattern creation abilities. These abilities also inform repetition, rhythm, categorization, and sequencing skills, which are important in math, music, art, literature, clothing design, etc.

Learning game that involves writing numbers, identifying numbers, and running
A game for young children that some educators call "Number Dash" (Miller, ed. Charner, 2009) builds foundational math concepts and skills, while providing physical activity. It can involve small or large groups (the referenced authors say "the more the merrier"). Help children write large numbers on a paved area with sidewalk chalk. Make sure numbers are spread far enough apart so children will not collide while running. There should be one of each number for each child (e.g., six "1s," "2s," "3s," etc. if there are six children). Use chalk colors that contrast with the pavement color to ensure the numbers will be highly visible. Tell children to run ("dash") to whichever number you call out and stand on it until you call another number. Call out numbers randomly. Encourage children who have located the number to help their classmates/playmates. This game develops gross motor skills, number writing skills, and number recognition skills. It also provides experience with playing organized games, following rules, following directions, and cooperating with and helping others. This game can also be played with letters, colors, and/or shapes.

Knowing number names and understanding 1:1 correspondence

Young children learn to name numbers in a way that is similar to how they learn to recite alphabet letters. However, learning to associate number symbols with concrete objects in the real world environment is a major advance in their cognitive development. The concept of 1:1 correspondence entails matching number symbols to the quantities they represent, an essential early math skill. Teachers can support the development of this math skill with a simple "grab bag" game youngsters enjoy. The teacher writes a number from 1 to 10 on each of ten cards, folding each card in half and putting them into a paper lunch bag. The teacher provides each child with a handful of pennies/play coins/buttons/little blocks to use as counting tokens. Each child takes a turn closing his/her eyes and pulling a card out of the bag. The child reads the number on the card, counts out the corresponding number of pennies/tokens, and puts them with the card. As children learn, teachers can place additional and/or different numbers (e.g., 11 to 20) in the grab bag. To promote the development of early literacy skills, teachers can also include the name of the number on each card.

Early math skills and sequencing/ practice fine motor skills

In hot weather, making ice cube necklaces is a fun activity that helps young children cool off while learning to sequence objects. The activity also helps children develop their manual motor skills and learn about liquid and solid states of matter. Regular ice cube trays are fine; those with "fun-shaped" compartments are even better. The teacher cuts plastic drinking straws so that they will fit into each ice cube compartment. The children participate, watching and/or helping pour water into trays and adding various food colorings/fruit juices. The teacher places one straw clipping into each compartment. While putting the trays into the freezer, the teacher tells children that 32° Fahrenheit/0° Celsius is the temperature at which water freezes. Children practice making scientific observations by noting how long the water takes to freeze. They empty the cubes into a big bowl. The children put on bathing suits or other clothing that can get wet, and the class goes outdoors. The teacher provides strings that are knotted at one end, and calls out a color pattern (e.g., one blue cube, then a yellow cube, etc.). Children follow the teacher's instructions to create color-patterned necklaces they can tie, wear, and watch melt.

Identifying shapes

The three levels of perceiving shapes that children typically move through sequentially are seeing, naming, and analyzing. Very young children recognize simple shapes like circles, squares, and triangles. As their cognitive and language skills develop, they learn the names for these shapes, and use these names to identify single shapes. The third level is analyzing each shape to understand its properties. Whereas identifying shapes visually is intuitive and based on association, analyzing their properties is more abstract, since a shape can have a number of different appearances. For example, three-year-olds can differentiate a triangle from other shapes. However, if you show them a very tall, skinny/short, wide/lopsided/crooked triangle, they will have trouble identifying it as a triangle. At the analysis level, children realize that a triangle has three sides, which are not necessarily equal in length. An activity that young children enjoy is closing their eyes, reaching into a bag of assorted shapes, finding a triangle by touch, and explaining why it is a triangle. This involves both the second and third levels of naming and analysis.

A significant mark of progress in early math skills development is the ability to not only identify various shapes, but also to draw them. Once young children develop this ability, they typically want to practice it all the time. Teachers can encourage this by helping children make pattern resist paintings. The teacher tapes white paper to children's tables/trays, gives them crayons, and invites them to fill the paper with drawings of different shapes of various sizes and colors. Teachers can introduce young children to new shapes (e.g., ovals, stars, crescent moons, etc.) by drawing them on separate pieces of paper for children to look at and copy. Then, the teacher replaces the crayons with water, watercolor paints, and brushes; shows the children how to dip brushes into paint and water to dilute the colors; and allows them to paint over their crayoned shapes, covering all the white paper with color. The children see the shapes show through the paint, creating the pattern resist. Dipping brushes and diluting various colors also develop children's color recognition skills and their hand-eye coordination.

Counting

A common practice among preschool children is counting on their fingers. Young children learn concretely before they develop abstract thought, so they must have concrete objects to work with to understand abstract mathematical concepts. They use their fingers to count because fingers are concrete. A simple activity that allows children to continue finger counting while removing additional visual support is "blind finger counting." Using eyesight to count objects we can see is relatively easy. However, when children cannot see objects, they must learn to count mentally instead. This allows them to take another step in their progress from concrete to abstract thinking. To count mentally without visual reinforcement takes practice. Teachers can tape a shoebox lid to the box and cut a small hole in it. Children can fit a hand through the hole, but cannot see inside. Children close their eyes; the teacher drops several small objects into the box; and each child reaches in, counting the objects using only touch. Varying objects and quantities maintains the fun of this activity.

Sorting and categorization

One of the major learning accomplishments of young children is being able to identify similarities and differences among objects. Developing this ability enables children to sort like objects into groups, and to place objects into categories based on their differences. When preschoolers compare and contrast objects, they demonstrate an important early step in the development of critical thinking, analytical, and problem solving skills. For an easy, entertaining guessing game, adults can select assorted household items familiar to children and put them into a bag/pillowcase. They then give children various clues (e.g., "I stir lemonade with this…," "It's made of wood," "We keep it in the kitchen drawer…," etc.) and ask them to guess which items are in the bag. It is important to give young children one to two minutes to consider each clue before they make a guess. Adults repeat clues when children guess incorrectly. If children guess correctly, they are allowed to look inside the bag. Youngsters greatly enjoy seeing that the object they guessed is actually inside the bag. Adults can gradually make the game more challenging by beginning with very common objects, and then eventually progressing to more unusual ones.

According to the U.S. Department of Agriculture, preschoolers need three ½-cup servings of fruit and three ½-cup servings of vegetables daily. However, many young children are picky/resistant. Adults can motivate them to eat produce with a "food rainbow" project. Adults show children a picture of a rainbow, and discuss its colors and their sequence (teaching some earth science, optics, and color theory!). A fun art project is allowing students to color their own rainbows, which improves fine motor skills. Then, adults can have children cut out pictures from grocery circulars and name each food. The adult can help children find one healthy fruit/vegetable for each color, gluing each food to its corresponding stripe on the rainbow. Adults can then help children pull apart cotton balls and glue them to their rainbow pictures to represent clouds. Children can then post their food rainbows on refrigerators as artwork and as healthy eating reminders. At the bottom, children can draw and color one box (bottom-up) for each food they eat (e.g., blue = blueberries, orange = carrots, red = apples, etc.) to create a bar graph. Children should try to "eat" the entire rainbow every week. This activity gives children the opportunity to produce colorful art, eat better, track and document their diets, and develop graphing skills.

Prerequisite abilities

Prerequisite abilities that young children need in order to develop early math skills include the ability to identify, copy, expand, and create patterns; as well as the ability to count. Adults can promote the development of these skills by giving children a craft project and introducing them to an interactive game they can play using their crafts. First, the children paint six ping pong balls red on one side to make red-and-white balls. Then, the children paint six ping pong balls blue on one side to make blue-and-white balls. Once the paint dries, the adult puts several balls into an egg carton so that one color is face up. The adult starts making a simple pattern (e.g., two white, then two red, then two blue), and asks each child to continue the pattern. Then, the adult allows each child to create his or her own original color patterns. Once a child masters creating patterns using solid colors, he or she can then use both the white and colored sides of the balls to create more complex patterns. Children can design an infinite number of patterns, which are often quite artistic.

<u>Developing counting skills, numeracy skills, and motor skills</u>
Young children enjoy tossing objects and practicing their aim. Adults can make a beanbag game that helps children learn numbers and identify sets, while also allowing them to construct their own game rules. First, the adult should cover five big, equally-sized coffee (or similar) cans with paper that is adhesive on one side. The adult should then use markers to write a number from 1 to 5 and draw the corresponding number of dots on each can. The next step is to fill 15 tube socks with beans and knot/tie/sew them shut. The following numerals and the corresponding number of dots should be written on each homemade beanbag using markers: the number 1 on five beanbags, the number 2 on four beanbags, the number 3 on three beanbags, the number 4 on two beanbags, and the number 5 on one beanbag. Next, the adult should attach the cans to the floor with tape or Velcro. Then, the adult should mark a line on the floor that children must stand behind, and should direct children ONLY to toss the beanbags into the cans. Children will devise various games/rules. First, they may simply toss the beanbags into the cans; then, some may try to toss beanbags into a can that has the same number as the one marked on the beanbag. Eventually, some may throw three beanbags into the "3" can. They may/may not keep score. Allowing children to determine the details and rules gives them an opportunity to develop their imagination and decision making skills, and to create their own games while learning number and set identification.

<u>Developing shape recognition skills, fine motor skills, creativity, observational skills, and general and early math vocabulary skills</u>

In one type of shape matching game, EC teachers help children make a game board out of construction paper that is shaped like a tree. Teachers first help the children cut a treetop and leaf shapes from green paper. They discuss children's preferences for tall/short and thick/thin trunks, giving them practice using descriptive vocabulary words, particularly ones related to size. This step builds both general and math concept vocabulary. Children cut trunks from brown paper and paste/glue them on the treetops. While out of the children's sight, the teacher cuts 5 to 10 (or more) pairs of shapes per child/tree from different colors of construction paper. Pairs should not match exactly (e.g., a blue square can be paired with a red square). The teacher glues one of each pair of shapes to each child's tree while the child is not looking. The teacher then gives each child the rest of the shapes, and invites children to see how quickly they can match each shape to its "partner" on the tree. The teacher can provide "warmer/cooler" distance clues, and should provide reinforcement each time a child correctly matches a pair of shapes. Teachers can make this activity more challenging by using more shapes and/or getting students to match shapes that are different sizes (e.g., children can be asked to match smaller diamonds to larger diamonds).

Strengthening numeracy skills

Adults can adapt the format of "20 Questions," "I Spy," and other similar guessing games to focus on numbers and help children learn number concepts. For example, adults could say, "I'm thinking of a number from 1 to 10…." and then give children 10 guesses. Adults give children cues as they guess, such as "higher" and "lower," to help them narrow down the number of possible correct answers. As children improve, adults can increase the number range (e.g., from 0 to 50) or use larger numbers (e.g., from 20 to 40). As children's skills and self-confidence develop, adults can reverse roles, having children think of numbers and give clues while adults guess. Young children enjoy the fun of guessing, getting closer using clues, deducing correct answers, and fooling adults with their own clues. Concurrently, they learn to describe numbers, compare them, and sequence them. Adults can make the game more difficult by limiting the number of guesses allowed and/or setting time limits. They can make it easier by providing a written number line for children to reference. This game requires no materials (or just a basic number line), is a great way to pass time, and entertains children while helping to develop numeracy skills.

Promoting pattern recognition skills, imagination, an understanding of symbolic representation, and map reading skills

A treasure hunt is an ideal outdoor activity for young children, and can also be adapted for indoor fun. The treasure can be anything (e.g., a small toy/play money/chocolate "coins"/rocks spray painted gold or silver, etc.). The adult should put the treasure in a paper bag marked with a large X. The adult should hide it somewhere where it is not visible, but will not be overly difficult for children to find. Then, the adult should make a treasure map, using few words and many pictures, sketching landmark objects in the area (trees, houses, etc. if the activity will be done outdoors, and furniture, walls, etc. if the activity will be done indoors). The adult should ensure the map is developmentally appropriate for young children, and that they will be able to read it independently. Adults with time and motivation can make the map look authentic by soaking it in tea/coffee, drying it in a 200° oven, or even charring its edges. Adults should include a dotted line on the map that reinforces the simple directions and indicates the path to the treasure, which is indicated on the map by a large X. Children have fun, use their imaginations, make connections between symbols and images to corresponding real-world physical objects, and begin learning to read maps.

Concept of starting at zero rather than one

A teacher is introducing standard measures to her class as part of a unit on measurement, one of the early math skills. She shows the children a ruler, explaining that it is one foot long, and that we can use it to measure inches and parts of inches. She demonstrates placing the ruler on paper to measure a given length, explaining that the ruler can also be used as a straight edge for drawing lines. One child asks, "How come you started with zero? Why don't you start with one like when we count?" The teacher responds, "That's a very good question! Zero means none/nothing. When we count, we start with one because we already have at least one of something. When you were born, you were not one year old; your age began at zero. After a year, on your first birthday, you were one year old. We also begin measuring distances at zero/none/nothing. The first piece/unit of measurement is one, not two. The distance from zero to one is equal to one. To get to one inch, for example, we need to start at zero."

Geometric shapes and their properties

A teacher has been working with students to help them develop their shape identification skills. They can recognize shapes by sight, and have also learned the defining properties of different shapes (number of sides, etc.). The teacher shows the class this figure:

She asks how many rectangles they can find in the figure. One student answers, "There is one rectangle," which is incorrect because a square is a rectangle; this figure has four rectangles that are squares. Moreover, the entire figure is itself a rectangle. Another student therefore says, "There are five rectangles." This response is also incorrect. Two adjacent squares also form a rectangle; this means there are three additional rectangles. Three adjacent squares also form a rectangle; this means there are two additional rectangles. Thus, the figure has a total of 10 rectangles. Solving this puzzle requires the use of many skills, including analyzing visual information, synthesizing visual information, recognizing patterns, recognizing shapes, and identifying the properties of shapes.

Collecting, organizing, and displaying data

A preschool teacher is teaching her group of ten children about basic data collection, data arrangement, and data display. She shows children yellow, blue, and green sticky notes, and has each child select his/her favorite color. Five children choose yellow notes, three select blue, and two choose green. By choosing one of three colors, each child has participated in data collection. The teacher draws lines to divide a sheet of paper into three columns, and labels each column with one of the colors. She helps the children place their chosen sticky notes in the correct columns. By arranging the colored sticky notes into columns, the teacher and children have organized the data they gathered. Once all notes are in their proper color columns, the completed chart is an example of how collected, organized data can be displayed.

<u>Selecting one of three colors of sticky notes, organizing them, and displaying them</u>
The teacher had ten children each choose one of three colors of sticky notes, an example of basic data collection. She used a chart with three columns to organize the children's choices as follows:

	yellow sticky note	
	yellow sticky note	
blue sticky note	yellow sticky note	
blue sticky note	yellow sticky note	green sticky note
blue sticky note	yellow sticky note	green sticky note
BLUE	YELLOW	GREEN

The chart displays the collected and organized data. The teacher asks the children which color was chosen the most. Seeing five yellow notes, they answer, "yellow." She asks which color was chosen the least, and they say, "green." She asks them to use numbers to arrange the color choices from most popular to least popular. They arrive at, "five yellow, three blue, and two green." Together, the teacher and the children point to and count ten children. She tells them five equals half of ten, and asks which color half of the children chose. Together, they figure out it was yellow. These are examples of analyzing and interpreting data.

Science

Fundamental science concepts

Science entails asking questions, conducting investigations, collecting data, and seeking answers to the questions asked by analyzing the data collected. Natural events that can be examined over time and student-centered inquiry through hands-on activities that require the application of problem solving skills are most appropriate for helping young children learn basic science. In their everyday lives, young children develop concepts of 1:1 correspondence through activities like fitting pegs into matching holes or distributing one item to each child in a class. They also develop counting concepts by counting enough items for each child in the group or counting pennies in a piggy bank. They develop classification concepts when they sort objects into separate piles according to their shapes or some other type of category (e.g., toy cars vs. toy trucks). When children transfer water, sand, rice, or other substances from one container to another, they develop measurement concepts. As they progress, children will apply these early concepts to more abstract scientific ideas during grade school.

Learning science as normal developmental processes

Infants use their senses to explore the environment, and are motivated by innate curiosity. As they develop mobility, children gain more freedom, allowing them to make independent discoveries and think for themselves. Children learn size concepts by comparing the sizes of objects/persons in the environment to their own size, and by observing that some objects are too large to hold, while others are small enough to hold. They learn about weight when trying to lift various objects. They learn about shape when they see that some objects roll away, while others do not. Babies learn temporal sequences when they wake up wet and hungry, cry, and have parents change and feed them. They also learn this concept by playing, getting tired, and going to sleep. As soon as they look and move around, infants learn about space, including large/small spaces. Eventually, they develop spatial sense through experiences like being put in a playpen/crib in the middle of a large room. Toddlers naturally sort objects into groups according to their sizes/shapes/colors/uses. They experiment with transferring water/sand among containers of various sizes. They learn part-to-whole relationships by building block structures and then dismantling them.

Naturalistic, informal, and structured learning experiences

Children actively construct their knowledge of the environment through exploring it. Young children's learning experiences can be naturalistic (i.e. spontaneously initiated by the child during everyday activities). During naturalistic learning, the child controls his/her choices and actions. Informal learning experiences also allow the child to choose his or her actions and activities, but they include adult intervention at some point during the child's engagement in naturalistic pursuits. In structured learning experiences, the adult chooses the activities and supplies some direction as to how the child should perform the associated actions. One consideration related to EC learning that teachers should keep in mind is that within any class or group of children, there are individual differences in learning styles. Additionally, children from different cultural groups have varying learning styles and approaches. EC teachers can introduce science content in developmentally appropriate ways by keeping these variations in mind.

Naturalistic learning experiences
Motivated by novelty and curiosity, young children spontaneously initiate naturalistic experiences during their everyday activities. Infants and toddlers in Piaget's sensorimotor stage learn by exploring the environment through their senses, so adults should provide them with many objects and substances they can see, hear, touch, smell, and taste. Through manipulating and observing concrete objects/substances, preschoolers in Piaget's preoperational stage begin learning concepts that will enable them to perform mental operations later on. Adults should observe children's actions and progress, and should give positive reinforcement in the form of looks, facial

expressions, gestures, and/or words encouraging and praising the child's actions. Young children need adult feedback to learn when they are performing the appropriate actions. For example, a toddler/preschooler selects a tool from the toolbox, saying, "This is big!" and the mother responds, "Yes!" A four-year-old sorting toys of various colors into separate containers is another example of a naturalistic experience. A five-year-old who observes while painting that mixing two colors yields a third color is yet another example.

Informal learning experience

Informal learning experiences involve two main components. First, the child spontaneously initiates naturalistic learning experiences during everyday activities to explore and learn about the environment. Second, the adult takes advantage of opportunities during naturalistic experiences to insert informal learning experiences. Adults do not plan these in advance, but take advantage of opportunities that occur naturally. One way this happens is when a child is on the right track to solve a problem, but needs some encouragement or a hint from the adult. Another way is when the adult spots a "teachable moment" during the child's naturalistic activity, and uses it to reinforce a basic concept. For example, a three-year-old might hold up three fingers, declaring, "I'm six years old." The parent says, "Let's count fingers: one, two, three. You're three years old." Or, a teacher asks a child who has a box of treats if s/he has enough for the whole class, and the child answers, "I don't know." The teacher then responds, "Let's count them together," and helps the child count.

Structured learning experiences

Naturalistic learning experiences are spontaneously initiated and controlled by children. Informal learning experiences involve unplanned interventions by adults during children's naturalistic experiences, which is when adults offer suitable correction/assistance/support. Structured learning experiences differ in that the adult pre-plans and initiates the activity/lesson, and provides the child with some direction. For example, a teacher who observes a four-year-old's need to practice counting can give the child a pile of toys, and then ask him/her how many there are. To develop size concepts, a teacher can give a small group of children several toys of different sizes, and then ask the children to inspect them and talk about their characteristics. The teacher holds up one toy, instructing children to find one that is bigger/smaller. If a child needs to learn shape concepts, the teacher might introduce a game involving shapes, giving the child instructions on how to play the game. Or, a first grade teacher, recognizing the importance of the concept of classification to the ability to organize scientific information, might ask students to bring in bones to classify during a unit on skeletons.

Activity collecting and organizing data

Preschoolers and kindergarteners continue their earlier practices of exploration to learn new things, and they apply fundamental science concepts to collect and organize data in order to answer questions. To collect data, children must have observation, counting, recording, and organization skills. One activity kindergarteners and teachers enjoy is growing bean sprouts. For example, the teacher can show children two methods: one using glass jars and paper towels saturated with water, the other using cups of dirt. The children add water daily as needed, observe developments, and report to the teacher, who records their observations on a chart. The teacher gives each child a chart that they add information to each day. The children count how many days their beans took to sprout in the glass jars and in the cups of dirt. They then compare their own results for the two methods, and they compare their results to those of their classmates. The children apply concepts of counting, numbers, time, 1:1 correspondence, and comparison of numbers. They also witness the planting and growing process.

Science process skills

Science process skills include observation (using the senses to identify properties of objects/situations), classification (grouping objects/situations according to their common properties), measurement (quantifying physical properties), communication (using observations, classifications, and measurements to report experimental results to others), inference (finding patterns and meaning in experiment results), and prediction (using experimental experience to formulate new hypotheses). Inferences and predictions must be differentiated from objective observations. Classification, measurement, and comparison are basic math concepts which, when applied to science problems, are called process skills. The other science process skills named, as well as defining and controlling variables, are equally necessary to solve both science and math problems. For example, using ramps can help young children learn basic physics concepts. Teachers ask children what would happen if two balls were rolled down a ramp at the same time, if two balls were rolled down a ramp of a different height/length, if two ramps of different heights/lengths were used, etc. In this activity, children apply the scientific concepts of observation, communication, inference, and prediction, as well as the concepts of height, length, counting, speed, distance, and comparison.

Scientific method

Children are born curious, and naturally engage in problem solving to learn. Problem solving and inquiry are natural child behaviors. EC teachers can use these behaviors to promote children's scientific inquiry. Scientific inquiry employs the scientific method. The first step in the method is to ask a question, which is another natural child behavior. Just as adult scientists formulate research questions, the first step of the scientific method for children is asking questions they want to answer. Next, to address a question, both adults and children must form a hypothesis (i.e. an educated guess about what the answer will be). The hypothesis informs and directs the next steps: designing and conducting an experiment to test whether the hypothesis is true or false. With teacher instruction/help, children experiment. For example, they might drop objects of different weights from a height to see when each lands, as Galileo did. Teachers help record outcomes. The next steps are deciding whether the results prove/disprove the hypothesis and reporting the results and conclusions to others.

Physical science and matter

Physical science is the study/science of the physical universe surrounding us. Everything in the universe consists of matter (i.e. anything that has mass and takes up space) or energy (i.e. anything that does not have mass or occupy space, but affects matter and space). Three states of matter are solid, liquid, and gas. Solids preserve their shape even when they are not in a container. Solids have specific, three-dimensional/crystalline atomic structures and specific melting points. Liquids have no independent shape outside of containers, but have specific volumes. Liquid molecules are less cohesive than solid molecules, but more cohesive than gas molecules. Liquids have flow, viscosity (flow resistance), and buoyancy. Liquids can undergo diffusion, osmosis, evaporation, condensation, solution, freezing, and heat conduction and convection. Liquids and gases are both fluids, and share some of the same properties. Gases have no shape, expanding and spreading indefinitely outside of containers. Gases can become liquid/solid through cooling/compression/both. Liquids/solids can become gaseous through heating. Vapor is the gaseous form of a substance that is solid/liquid at lower temperatures. For example, when water is heated it becomes steam, a vapor.

Solids

Solids are one of the three forms of matter. The other two are liquids and gases. *Solids* maintain their shape when they are not inside of containers, whereas liquids and gases acquire the shapes of containers holding them. Containers also prevent liquids and gases from dispersing. Of the three forms of matter, solids have the most cohesive molecules. Solid molecules are most attracted to each other, and solid molecules are held together most strongly. Solid atoms are organized into defined, three-dimensional, lattice-shaped patterns (i.e. they are crystalline in structure). Solids also have specific temperatures at which they melt. Some substances that seem solid, such as plastic, gel, tar, and glass, are actually not true solids. They are amorphous solids because their atoms do not have a crystalline structure, but are amorphous (i.e. the positions of their atoms have no long-range organization). They also have a range of melting temperatures rather than specific melting points.

Liquids

Of the three states of matter—solid, liquid, and gas—*liquids* have properties that fall somewhere in between those of solids and gases. The molecules of solids are the most cohesive (i.e. they have the greatest mutual attraction). Gas molecules are the least cohesive, and liquid molecules are in between. Liquids have no definite shape, while solids do. Liquids have a definite volume, whereas gases do not. The cohesion of liquid molecules draws them together, and the molecules below the surface pull surface molecules down, creating surface tension. This property can be observed in containers of water. Liquid molecules are also attracted to other substance's molecules (i.e. adhesion). Surface tension and adhesion combined cause liquids to rise in narrow containers, a property known as capillarity. Liquids are buoyant (i.e. they exert upward force so objects which have more buoyancy than weight float in liquids, while objects which have more weight than buoyancy sink in liquids). Liquids can be made solid by freezing, and can be made gaseous by heating/evaporation. Liquids can diffuse, which means they can mix with other molecules. Liquid diffusion across semi-permeable membranes is known as osmosis.

Gases

Gas, liquid, and solid are the three states of matter. *Gases* have the least cohesive (i.e. mutually attracted) molecules of the three states of matter, while solids have the most cohesive molecules. Gases do not maintain a defined shape, while solids do. If not contained within a receptacle, gases spread and expand indefinitely. Gases can be elementary or compound. An elementary gas is composed of only one kind of chemical element. At normal temperatures and pressures, 12 elementary gases are known: argon*, chlorine, fluorine, helium*, hydrogen, krypton*, neon*, nitrogen, oxygen, ozone, radon*, and xenon*. Compound gases have molecules containing atoms of more than one kind of chemical element. Carbon monoxide (which contains one carbon and one oxygen atom) and ammonia (which contains nitrogen and hydrogen atoms) are common compound gases. Heating gas molecules/atoms charges them electrically, making them ions. Plasma combines positive gas ions and electrons. Some gases are colorless and odorless, while others are not. Some burn with oxygen, while others do not. *Noble/inert gases have single atoms that do not normally form compounds with other elements.

Light

When a beam of light hits a smooth surface like a mirror, it bounces back off that surface. This rebounding is reflection. In physics, the law of reflection states that "the angle of incidence equals the angle of reflection." This means that when light is reflected, it always bounces off the surface at the same angle at which it hit that surface. When a beam of light hits a rough rather than a smooth surface, though, it is reflected back at many different angles, not just the angle at which it struck the surface. This reflection at multiple and various angles is scattering. Many objects we commonly use every day have rough surfaces. For example, paper may look smooth to the naked eye, but actually has a rough surface. This property can be observed by viewing paper through a microscope. Because light waves striking paper are reflected in every direction by its rough surface, scattering enables us to read words printed on paper from any viewing angle.

When light strikes a medium, the light wave's frequency is equal or close to the frequency at which the electrons in the medium's atoms can vibrate. These electrons receive the light's energy, making them vibrate. When a medium's atoms hang on tightly to their electrons, the electrons transmit their vibrations to the nucleus of each atom. This makes the atoms move faster and collide with the medium's other atoms. The energy the atoms got from the vibrations is then released as heat. This process is known as absorption of light. Materials that absorb light, such as wood and metal, are opaque. Some materials absorb certain light frequencies but transmit others. For example, glass transmits visible light (and therefore appears transparent to the naked eye), but absorbs ultraviolet frequencies. The sky looks blue because the atmosphere absorbs all colors in the spectrum except blue, which it reflects. Only blue wavelengths/frequencies bounce back to our eyes. This is an example of subtractive color, which we see in paints/dyes and all colored objects/materials. Pigments absorb some frequencies and reflect others.

When light moves from one transparent medium to another (e.g., between water and air/vice versa), the light's speed changes, bending the light wave. It bends either away from or toward the normal line, an imaginary straight line running at right angles to the medium's surface. We easily observe this bending when looking at a straw in a glass of water. The straw appears to break/bend at the waterline. The angle of refraction is the amount that the light wave bends. It is determined by how much the medium slows down the light's speed, which is the medium's refraction index. For example, diamonds are much denser and harder than water, and thus have a higher refraction index. They slow down and trap light more than water does. Consequently, diamonds sparkle more than water. Lenses, such as those in eyeglasses and telescopes, rely on the principle of refraction. Curved lenses disperse or concentrate light waves, refracting light as it both enters and exits, thus changing the light's direction. This is how lenses correct (eyeglasses) and enhance (telescopes) our vision.

Magnetism

Magnetism is the property some objects/substances have of attracting other materials. The form of magnetism most familiar to us is certain materials attracting iron. Magnets also attract steel, cobalt, and other materials. Generators supplying power include magnets, as do all electric motors. Loudspeakers and telephones contain magnets. Tape recorders use magnets. The tape they play is magnetized. Magnets are used in compasses to determine the location of north and various corresponding directions. In fact, the planet Earth is itself a giant magnet (which is why compasses point north). Hence, like the Earth, all magnets have two poles: a north/north-seeking pole and a south/south-seeking pole. Opposite poles attract, and like poles repel each other. Magnets do not need to touch to attract/repel each other. A magnet's effective area/range is its magnetic field. All materials have some response to magnetic fields. Magnets make nearby magnetic materials into magnets, a process known as magnetic induction. Materials that line up parallel to magnetic force field lines are paramagnetic, while materials that line up perpendicular to magnetic force field lines are diamagnetic.

Scientists have known about the effects of magnetism for hundreds of years. However, they do not know exactly what magnetism is, or what causes it. French physicist Pierre Weiss proposed a theory of magnetism in the early 20th century that is widely accepted. This theory posits that every magnetic material has groups of molecules—domains—that function as magnets. Until a material is magnetized, its domains have a random arrangement, so one domain's magnetism is cancelled out by another's. When the material comes into a magnetic field—the range/area wherein a magnet is effective—its domains align themselves parallel to the magnetic field's lines of force. As a result, all of their north-seeking/north poles point in the same direction. Removing the magnetic field causes like poles to repel one another as they normally do. In easily magnetized materials, domains revert to random order. In materials that are harder to magnetize, domains lack sufficient force to disassemble, leaving the material magnetized. Later versions of Weiss's theory attribute domain magnetism to spinning electrons.

Electrical properties of insulation and conduction in terms of atomic structure

The smallest units of all matter are atoms. The nuclei of atoms are orbited by negatively charged electrons. Some materials have electrons that are strongly bound to their atoms. These include air, glass, wood, cotton, plastic, and ceramic. Since their atoms rarely release electrons, these materials have little or no ability to conduct electricity, and are known as electrical insulators. Insulators resist/block conduction. Metals and other conductive materials have free electrons that can detach from the atoms and move around. Without the tight binding of insulators, materials with loose electrons enable electric current to flow easily through them. Such materials are called electrical conductors. The movements of their electrons transmit electrical energy. Electricity requires something to make it flow (i.e. a generator). A generator creates a steady flow of electrons by moving a magnet close to a wire, creating a magnetic field to propel electrons. Electricity also requires a conductor (i.e. a medium through which it can move from one place to another).

Electrical current and current/amperage and voltage

Magnetism and electricity are related, and they interact with each other. Generators work by using magnets near conductive wires to produce moving streams of electrons. The agent of movement can range from a hand crank, to a steam engine, to the nuclear fission process. However, all agents of movements operate according to the same principle. A simple analogy is that a generator magnetically pushes electrical current the way a pump pushes water. Just as water pumps apply specific amounts of pressure to specific numbers of water molecules, generator magnets apply specific amounts of "pressure" to specific numbers of electrons. The number of moving electrons in an electrical circuit equals the current, or amperage. The unit of measurement for amperage is the ampere, or amp. The amount of force moving the electrons is the voltage. Its unit of measurement is the volt. One amp equals 6.24×10^{18} electrons passing through a wire each second. For example, a generator could produce 1 amp using 6 volts when rotating 1,000 times per minute. Today's power stations rely on generators.

Heat

Heat is transmitted through conduction, radiation, and convection. Heat is transmitted in solids through conduction. When two objects at different temperatures touch each other, the hotter object's molecules are moving faster. They collide with the colder object's molecules, which are moving slower. As a result of the collision, the molecules that are moving more rapidly supply energy to the molecules that are moving more slowly. This speeds up the movement of the (previously) slower moving molecules, which heats up the colder object. This process of transferring heat through contact is called thermal conductivity. An example of thermal conductivity is the heat sink. Heat sinks are used in many devices. Today, they are commonly used in computers. A heat sink transfers the heat building up in the computer processor, moving it away before it can damage the processor. Computers contain fans, which blow air across their heat sinks and expel the heated air out of the computers.

Vibrations and sound

When any physical object moves back and forth rapidly, this is known as vibration. The movements that occur during vibration disturb the surrounding medium, which may be solid, liquid, or gaseous. The most common sound conducting medium in our environment is gaseous: our atmosphere (i.e. the air). An object's vibratory movements represent a form of energy. As this acoustic energy moves through the air, it takes the form of waves, sound waves specifically. The outer ear receives and amplifies the sound and transmits it to the middle ear, where tiny bones vibrate in response to the sound energy and transmit it to the inner ear. The inner ear converts the acoustic energy into electrical energy. The electrical impulses are then carried by nerves to the brain. Structures in the brain associated with hearing receive these electrical signals and interpret them (i.e. make sense of them) as sounds. The ears' reception of sound waves is auditory sensation, and the brain's interpretation of them is auditory perception.

Positions and motions of objects in space in the physical world

Moving physical objects changes their positions. According to Newton's first law of motion, an object at rest tends to stay at rest and an object in motion tends to stay in motion, unless/until an opposing force changes the object's state of rest/motion. For example, an object at rest could be a small rock sitting on the ground. If you kick the rock into the air, it moves through the air. The rock will continue to move, but when a force like gravity acts on it, it falls/stops moving. The resulting motion from kicking the rock illustrates Newton's third law of motion: for every action there is an equal and opposite reaction. The acceleration or increase in velocity (a) of an object depends on its mass (m) and the amount of force (F) that is applied to the object. Newton's second law of motion states that F = ma (force equals mass times acceleration). Thus, moving objects maintain their speeds unless some force(s) cause acceleration or slowing/stopping, as frictional forces do.

Solar system's location and components

The universe is composed of an unknown (possibly infinite) number of galaxies or star systems, such as the Spiral Nebula, the Crab Nebula, and the Milky Way. Our sun, Sol, is one of billions of stars in the Milky Way. The solar system's planets are held in position at varying distances (according to their size and mass) from the Sun by its gravitational force. These planets orbit or revolve around the Sun. From the closest to the Sun to the farthest away, the solar system's planets are Mercury, Venus, Earth, Mars, Jupiter, Saturn, Uranus, and Neptune. Pluto was historically included as the ninth planet, but was demoted to a "dwarf planet" by the International Astronomical Union in 2006. Due to angular momentum, planets rotate on their axes, which are imaginary central lines between their north and south poles. One complete Earth rotation equals what we perceive as one 24-hour day. As the Earth turns, different portions face the Sun. These receive daylight, while the portions turned away from the Sun are in darkness. One complete revolution of the Earth around the Sun represents one calendar year.

Pluto

Since more powerful observatories have enabled greater detection and measurement of celestial objects, the International Astronomical Union has defined three criteria for defining a planet. First, it must orbit the Sun. Pluto meets this criterion. Second, it must have enough gravitational force to shape itself into a sphere. Pluto also meets this criterion. Third, a planet must have "cleared the neighborhood" in its orbit. This expression refers to the fact that as planets form, they become the strongest gravitational bodies within their orbits. Therefore, when close to smaller bodies, planets either consume these smaller bodies or repel them because of their greater gravity, clearing their orbital area/"neighborhood." To do this, a planet's mass must sufficiently exceed the mass of other bodies in its orbit. Pluto does not meet this criterion, having only 0.07 times the mass of other objects within its orbit. Thus, astronomers reclassified Pluto as a "dwarf planet" in 2006 based on its lesser mass and the many other objects in its orbit with comparable masses and sizes.

Earth

Earth is roughly spherical in shape. Its North and South Poles at the top and bottom are farthest away from and least exposed to the Sun, so they are always coldest. This accounts for the existence of the polar ice caps. The Equator, an imaginary line running around Earth at its middle exactly halfway between the North and South Poles, is at 0° latitude. Sunrises and sunsets at the Equator are the world's fastest. Days and nights are of virtually equal length at the Equator, and there is less seasonal variation than in other parts of the world. The equatorial climate is a tropical rainforest. Locations close to the North Pole, like Norway, are at such high latitudes that their nights are not dark in summertime, hence the expression "Land of the Midnight Sun." They also have very little light in wintertime. As Earth revolves around the Sun over the course of a year, the distance and angle of various locations relative to the Sun change, so different areas receive varying amounts of heat and light. This is what accounts for the changing seasons.

Rocks found on the Earth's surface

Earth's rock types are sedimentary, igneous, and metamorphic. These categories are based on the respective processes that form each type of rock. Igneous rocks are formed from volcanoes. Metamorphic rocks are formed when igneous and sedimentary rocks deep inside the Earth's crust are subjected to intense heat and/or pressure. Sedimentary rocks are formed on Earth's surface, and characteristically accumulate in layers. Erosion and other natural processes deposit these layers. Some sedimentary rocks are held together by electrical attraction. Others are cemented together by chemicals and minerals that existed during their formation. Still others are not held together at all, but are loose and crumbly. There are three subcategories of sedimentary rock. Clastic sedimentary rocks are made of little rock bits—clasts—that are compacted and cemented together. Chemical sedimentary rocks are frequently formed through repeated flooding and subsequent evaporation. The evaporation of water leaves a layer of minerals that were dissolved in the water. Limestone and deposits of salt and gypsum are examples. Organic sedimentary rocks are formed from organic matter, such as the calcium left behind from animal bones and shells.

Earth's metamorphic rocks

Sedimentary rocks are formed on the Earth's surface by layers of eroded material from mountains that were deposited by water, minerals like lime, salt and gypsum deposited by evaporated floodwater, and organic material like calcium from animal bones and shells. Igneous rocks are formed from liquid volcanic rock—either magma underground or lava on the surface—that cools and hardens. Metamorphic rocks are formed from sedimentary and igneous rocks. This happens when sedimentary and/or igneous rocks are deep inside the Earth's crust, where they are subjected to great pressure or heat. The process of metamorphism does not melt these rocks into liquid, which would happen inside a volcano. Rather, the pressure and/or heat change the rocks' molecular structure. Metamorphic rocks are thus more compact and denser than the sedimentary or igneous rocks from which they were formed. They also contain new minerals produced either by the reconfiguration of existing minerals' structures or by chemical reactions with liquids infiltrating the rock. Two examples of metamorphic rocks are marble and gneiss.

Igneous rocks

Igneous or volcanic rocks are formed from the magma emitted when a volcano erupts. Magma under the Earth's surface is subject to heat and pressure, keeping it in liquid form. During a volcanic eruption, some magma reaches the surface, emerging as lava. Lava cools rapidly in the outside air, becoming a solid with small crystals. Some magma does not reach Earth's surface, but is trapped underground within pockets in other rocks. Magma cools more slowly underground than lava does on the surface. This slower cooling forms rocks with larger crystals and coarser grains. The chemical composition and individual cooling temperatures of magma produce different kinds of igneous rocks. Lava that cools rapidly on the Earth's surface can become obsidian, a smooth, shiny black glass without crystals. It can also become another type of extrusive rock, such as andesite, basalt, pumice, rhyolite, scoria, or tuff (formed from volcanic ash and cinders). Magma that cools slowly in underground pockets can become granite, which has a coarse texture and large, visible mineral grains. It can also become another type of intrusive rock, such as diorite, gabbro, pegmatite, or peridotite.

Erosion

Erosion is a natural process whereby Earth's landforms are broken down through weathering. Rain, wind, etc. wear away solid matter. Over time, rain reduces mountains to hills. Rocks break off from mountains, and in turn disintegrate into sand. Weathering and the resulting erosion always occur in downhill directions. Rain washes rocks off mountains and down streams. Rains, rivers, and streams wash soils away, and ocean waves break down adjacent cliffs. Rocks, dirt, and sand change their form and location through erosion. They do not simply vanish. These transformations and movements are called mass wasting, which occurs chemically (as when rock is dissolved by chemicals in water) or mechanically (as when rock is broken into pieces). Because materials travel as a result of mass wasting, erosion can both break down some areas and build up others. For example, a river runs through and erodes a mountain, carrying the resulting sediment downstream. This sediment gradually builds up, creating wetlands at the river's mouth. A good example of this process is Louisiana's swamps, which were created by sediment transported by the Mississippi River.

Basic physical characteristics of living organisms

All living organisms have fundamental needs that must be met. For example, plants that grow on land need light, air, water, and nutrients in amounts that vary according to the individual plant. Undersea plants may need less/no light. They need gases present in the water, but not in the air above the water. Like land plants, they require nutrients. Like plants, animals (including humans) need air, water, and nutrients. They do not depend on light for photosynthesis like most plants, but some animals require more light than others, while others need less than others or none at all. Organisms cannot survive in environments that do not meet their basic needs. However, many organisms have evolved to adapt to various environments. For example, cacti are desert plants that thrive with only tiny amounts of water, and camels are desert animals that can also go for long periods of time with little water. Penguins and polar bears have adapted to very cold climates. Internal cues (e.g., hunger) and external cues (e.g., environmental change) motivate and shape the behaviors of individual organisms.

Animal life cycles

Most animals, including mammals, birds, fish, reptiles, and spiders, have simple life cycles. They are born live or hatch from eggs, and then grow to adulthood. Animals with simple life cycles include humans. Amphibians like frogs and newts have an additional stage involving a metamorphosis, or transformation. After birth, they breathe through gills and live underwater during youth (e.g., tadpoles). By adulthood, they breathe through lungs and move to land. Butterflies are examples of animals (insects) that undergo complete metamorphosis, meaning they change their overall form. After hatching from an embryo/egg, the juvenile form, or larva, resembles a worm and completes the majority of feeding required. In the next stage, the pupa does not feed, and is typically camouflaged in what is called an inactive stage. Mosquito pupae are called tumblers. The butterfly pupa is called a chrysalis, and is protected by a cocoon. In the final stage, the adult (imago) grows wings (typically) and breeds. Some insects like dragonflies, cockroaches, and grasshoppers undergo an incomplete metamorphosis. There are egg, larva, and adult stages, but no pupa stage.

Reproduction

A few examples of the many ways in which organisms reproduce include binary fission, whereby the cells of prokaryotic bacteria reproduce; budding, which is how yeast cells reproduce; and asexual reproduction. The latter occurs in plants when they are grafted, when cuttings are taken from them and then rooted, or when they put out runners. Plants also reproduce sexually, as do humans and most other animals. Animals, including humans, produce gametes (i.e. sperm or eggs) in their gonads through the process of meiosis. Gametes are haploid, containing half the number of chromosomes found in the body's cells. During fertilization, the gametes combine to form a zygote, which is diploid. It has the full number of chromosomes (half from each gamete), which are arranged in a genetically unique combination. Zygotes undergo mitosis, reproducing their gene combination with identical DNA sequences in all new cells, which then migrate and differentiate into organizations of specialized organs and tissues. These specialized organs in biologically mature organisms, alerted by signals such as hormonal cues, undergo meiosis to create new haploid gametes, beginning the cycle again.

Plant reproduction

Most plants can reproduce asexually. For example, cuttings can be rooted in water and planted. Some plants put out runners that root new growths. Many plants can be grafted to produce new ones. Plants also reproduce sexually. Plants' sexual life cycles are more complex than animals', since plants alternate between haploid form (i.e. having a single set of chromosomes) and diploid form (i.e. having two sets of chromosome) during their life cycles. Plants produce haploid cells called gametes* (equivalent to sperm and egg in animals) that combine during fertilization, producing zygotes (diploid cells with chromosomes from both gametes). Cells reproduce exact copies through mitosis (asexual reproduction), becoming differentiated/specialized to form organs. Mature diploid plants called sporophytes—the plant form we usually see—produce spores. In sporophytes' specialized organs, cells undergo meiosis. This is part of the process of sexual reproduction, during which cells with half the normal number of chromosomes are produced before fertilization occurs. The spores produced by the sporophyte generation undergo mitosis, growing into a haploid plant of the gametophyte generation that produces gametes*. The cycle then repeats.

Ecology

Ecology is defined as the study of interactions between organisms and their environments. Abiotic factors are the parts of any ecosystem that are not alive, but which affect that ecosystem's living members. Abiotic factors also determine the locations of particular ecosystems that have certain characteristics. Abiotic factors include the sunlight; the atmosphere, including oxygen, hydrogen, and nitrogen; the water; the soil; the temperatures within a system; and the nutrient cycles of chemical elements and compounds that pass among living organisms and their physical environments. Biotic factors are the living organisms within any ecosystem, which include not only humans and animals, but also plants, microorganisms, etc. The definition of biotic factors also includes the interactions that occur between and among various organisms within an ecosystem. Sunlight determines plant growth and, hence, biome locations. Sunlight, in turn, is affected by water depth. Ocean depths where sunlight penetrates, called photic zones, are where the majority of the photosynthesis on Earth occurs.

Ecological relationship

Organisms interact, both with other organisms and their environments. Relationships wherein two differing organisms regularly interact so that one or both of them benefit are known as ecological relationships. In mutualistic relationships, both organisms benefit. For example, bacteria live in termites' digestive systems. Termites eat wood. However, they cannot digest the cellulose (the main part of plant cell walls) in wood. The bacteria in termites' guts break down the cellulose for them, releasing the wood's nutrients. Reciprocally, the termites as hosts give the bacteria a home and food. In commensalistic relationships, one organism benefits and the other one is unaffected. One example is barnacles attaching to whales. Barnacles, which are filter feeders, benefit from the whales' swimming, which creates currents in the water that bring the barnacles food. The whales are not disturbed by the barnacles. In parasitic relationships, the parasite benefits, but the host suffers. For example, tapeworms inside animals' digestive tracts get nutrients. The hosts lose the nutrients stolen by the worms, and can sustain tissue damage because of the presence of the tapeworms.

Health and Physical Education

Promoting human health and wellness and preventing disease

Health and disease prevention begin before birth. Expecting mothers need to be/become informed about good nutrition for all humans and the supplemental nutrition required for prenatal support of developing embryos and fetuses. Mothers also need to get sufficient but not overly strenuous exercise; avoid undue stress; have/learn effective coping skills to deal with unavoidable life stressors; and avoid exposure to environmental toxins, such as radiation, pollution, and chemicals. They should avoid alcohol, tobacco, and exposure to secondhand smoke, as well as most drugs—street, over-the-counter, herbal, and prescription—unless they are prescribed by obstetricians/other physicians who are aware of the pregnancy. Babies initially need their mother's colostrum to provide immunity, and subsequently require breast milk or approved infant formula. Babies must also be held, cuddled, and given attention and affection to ensure survival, growth, and health. Young children need smaller amounts of food than adults that is equally as nutritious; sufficient exercise; adequate sleep; and cognitive, emotional, and social stimulation and interaction. Appropriate nutrition and exercise, avoidance of alcohol/tobacco/other drugs, and positive relationships and interactions are essential for wellness and disease prevention at all ages.

American Recovery and Reinvestment Act

The 2009 American Recovery and Reinvestment Act has allotted $650 million for preventing chronic disease. To apply these funds, the U.S. Department of Health and Human Services (HHS) has designed a comprehensive initiative entitled Communities Putting Prevention to Work. This initiative aims to create sustainable positive health changes in American communities, prevent or delay chronic disease, reduce disease risk factors, and promote child and adult wellness. Obesity and tobacco use, considered the foremost preventable sources of disability and death, are targeted by this initiative's evidence-based research programs and strategies, which are intended to reinforce state abilities and mobilize community resources. The initiative's central, $373-million community program includes support from the Centers for Disease Control and Prevention in selected communities for attaining the prevention outcomes of increasing physical activity levels, improving nutrition, reducing the incidence of obesity and higher than optimal body weights, decreasing tobacco use, and decreasing secondhand smoke exposure. Through this initiative, HHS hopes to produce effective models that can be reproduced in states and communities nationwide.

Federal Executive Order 13045

Passed by President Clinton, Executive Order 13045 declares a policy for identifying and assessing environmental health and safety risks that affect children disproportionately, and for addressing these risks through the policies, standards, programs, and activities of every independent federal regulatory agency. This order defines environmental health and safety risks as those that can be attributed to substances children ingest or contact (e.g., air they breathe; food they eat; water they drink, bathe in, and swim in; soil they live upon; and products they are exposed to or use). The order established a task force reporting to the president and consulting with the Domestic Policy Council, the National Science and Technology Council, the Council on Environmental Quality, and the Office of Management and Budget. The task force is co-chaired by the HHS secretary and the EPA administrator. The task force oversees a coordinated, integrated federal research agenda and reports relevant research/data biennially; issues principle, policy, and priority statements; recommends appropriate federal/state/local/tribal government, nonprofit, and private sector partnerships; makes public outreach/communication proposals; identifies related high-priority initiatives; and evaluates new legislation to determine whether it will meet the goals of Executive Order 13045.

Environmental health risks for children

Children's body systems, unlike those of mature adults, are still developing. They eat, drink, and breathe more in proportion to their body sizes than adults do. Typical child behaviors expose children to more potentially toxic chemicals and organisms. Therefore, children can be more vulnerable to environmental health risks. To protect children, adults can prohibit smoking in homes and cars; keep homes free of dust, mold, pet dander, and pests that can trigger allergies; avoid outdoor activities on high-pollution/"ozone alert" days; and carpool and/or use public transportation. Adults can prevent lead poisoning by only giving children cold water to drink and using cold water to prepare infant formula and cook food; washing bottles, pacifiers, and toys frequently; and protecting children from lead-based paints in older buildings. Adults must ensure children do not have access to toxic chemicals. Maintaining furnaces, chimneys, and appliances; using outdoor gas appliances and tools properly; refraining from using gas appliances and tools indoors; and installing approved CO alarms can all help prevent carbon monoxide poisoning. Choosing fish carefully can help prevent mercury toxicity. Keeping infants out of direct sunlight, using sun-protective clothing, and applying sunscreen on young children are also important.

Physical, emotional, and social factors

The parts of the body, including the brain, are connected, related, interactive, and interdependent. As humans also interact and are interdependent with their environment, both internal and external factors influence their health. For example, physical factors like exposure to air pollution or radiation can cause illnesses like asthma, other lung diseases, and various cancers. Too much or too little nutrition can cause obesity and diabetes* or malnutrition. Too much or too little exercise can cause exhaustion and injuries or weakness, diabetes*, and cardiovascular and pulmonary problems. Not exercising enough may also be a factor in being overweight or obese. *Diabetes itself causes many related health problems, including blindness, circulatory deficiencies, amputation, and cardiovascular disease. Water and/or sleep deprivation ultimately cause death. Emotional factors like depression, anxiety, and irritability can cause a host of health problems, including insomnia, overeating, anorexia, high blood pressure, and heart disease. Social factors include family influences. According to the family systems theory, dysfunctional family dynamics can cause a child to develop a physical illness. Whether the source is family, society outside the home, or both, stress is a social influence with multiple negative health impacts.

Nutrition

Children must consume a full range of nutrients for their brains to work normally. They need protein for its amino acids, which enable the brain's neurotransmitters (chemical messengers) to fire and communicate with each other. They need fruit and vegetable sugars and other complex carbohydrates to supply fuel to power the brain's functioning. Children's nutrition begins before birth. Pregnant women who do not eat adequate nutrients, vitamins, and minerals have higher risks of delivering infants with low birth weights. Research has found that babies with low birth weights are more likely to experience hearing and vision problems, and to need special education services in school at some point. Children in school who consume insufficient amounts of protein have been found to score lower on achievement tests than their peers who are getting enough protein. Children with iron deficiencies display fatigue and ADHD-like symptoms, including impaired concentration, shortened attention spans, and irritability. Children who miss breakfast consistently perform slower on problem solving tests than those who do not. Their responses are also less accurate. Children who regularly miss meals have compromised immunity against illnesses and infections, and they miss more school.

Motor skills

Motor skills are the large and small movements of the body. These movements include such things as pushing, pulling, lifting, and carrying larger objects using the legs, arms, and back; and picking up, grasping, and manipulating smaller objects using the hands and fingers. The former are gross motor skills, and the latter are fine motor skills. To develop these, children must make effective use of their mind-body connection (i.e. getting the muscles and bones to perform the movements the mind intends). They must also have developed spatial awareness (i.e. an accurate sense of the relationship between their bodies and the surrounding space and other bodies/objects). Teaching children to move large and small muscles in time to rhythmic songs helps develop motor skills. Teaching directions like up, down, clockwise, counterclockwise, etc. helps with motor planning development. When children find motor skills challenging to master, educators must provide them with frequent instruction, adequate re-teaching, and ample modeling that allows them to observe and imitate problematic movements.

Newborn motor reflexes

Newborns exhibit the tonic reflex, adopting the "fencing position." In this position, the head is turned to one side, the arm on that side is in front of the eyes, and the other arm is flexed. This normally disappears by the time an infant is around four months old. It may serve as preparation for reaching voluntarily for things/people. The stepping reflex disappears at around two months of age, and prepares babies for walking voluntarily. The palmar grasping reflex on an adult finger disappears by the time an infant is around three to four months old, and prepares babies for grasping voluntarily. When held upright, a baby can typically hold his/her head steady and erect by about six weeks of age on average. About 90 percent of infants will develop this skill between the ages of three weeks and four months. Babies lift up from the prone position using their arms by the time they are about two months old. About 90 percent of infants will develop this skill between the ages of three weeks and four months. Babies can also roll from side to back by the time they are about two months old. About 90 percent of infants will develop this skill between the ages of three weeks and five months. An infant can grasp a cube by the age of three months and three weeks on average. About 90 percent of infants will develop this skill between the ages of two and seven months.

Motor skills milestones - infants
By four and a half months on average, babies can roll from back to side. The range within which 90 percent of infants will be able to do this is two to seven months. Most babies can sit unsupported by seven months on average. The range within which 90 percent of infants will be able to do this is five to nine months. Most infants also crawl by seven months on average. The range within which 90 percent of infants will be able to do this is five to eleven months. Babies pull themselves up to a standing position by around eight months on average. The range within which 90 percent of infants will be able to do this is five to twelve months. Babies play "patty-cake" by nine months, three weeks on average. The range within which 90 percent of infants will be able to do this is seven to fifteen months. Babies/toddlers can stand alone by 11 months on average. The range within which 90 percent of infants will be able to do this is 9 to 16 months. Toddlers can walk unassisted by the age of 11 months, 3 weeks on average. The range within which 90 percent of infants will be able to do this is 9 to 17 months. Children can stack two cubes by the age of 13 months, 3 weeks on average. The range within which 90 percent of infants will be able to do this is 10 to 19 months. They scribble energetically by the age of 14 months on average. The range within which 90 percent of infants will be able to do this is 10 to 21 months. They can climb stairs with assistance by the age of 16 months on average. The range within which 90 percent of infants will be able to do this is 12 to 23 months. Normally developing children can typically can jump in place by the age of 23 months, 2 weeks on average. The range within which 90 percent of infants will be able to do this is 17 to 30 months.

Motor skills milestones - preschool children

Children develop motor skills most quickly between the ages of two and six years. They demonstrate basic locomotion skills, first walking and then running, skipping, hopping, galloping, and jumping. They also develop ball-handling skills, fine motor eye-hand coordination, and—as an extension of previously developed creeping skills—climbing skills. By two years of age, children develop balance for basic kicking, which evolves into the ability to execute full kicks (including backswings) by six years of age. They try throwing by two to three years of age. They develop related skills—including taking a forward step—by the age of six. They develop the ability to shuffle by three years of age, which develops into the ability to skip by six years of age. By the age of three, children walk automatically. They try running, but they are clumsy and lack adequate control. This ability improves by between four and five years of age. By this time, children are also more skilled at executing starts, stops, and turns. By the age of five or six, children can run like adults. They develop climbing skills (ladders, etc.) between the ages of three and six. The ability to jump longer distances and hopping and galloping skills develop by age six. Children can catch a large ball while holding their arm straight by the age of three. They can catch a ball while holding their elbows out to the front by age four, and they can do this while holding their elbows at their sides by age six.

Gross motor skills

The first motor movements of EC are gross motor skills (i.e. large body movements involving the torso, limbs, and feet). Sitting, standing, crawling, walking, running, galloping, jumping, catching, throwing, and kicking use these skills. Activities that help young children develop their gross motor skills include standing on dots/marks on the floor/ground; crawling under and climbing over things, including objects that are part of obstacle courses; and balancing on balance beams. These develop body control, coordination, laterality (using the left/right sides of the body separately), and synchronization of the body's left and right sides. Children develop body control and balance through hopping around objects. They develop coordination and overall gross motor skills through jumping over things like boxes, beanbags, lines/strings; and by kicking balls, balloons, etc. of various sizes. Walking and running around, through, and/or over obstacles like tires, hoops, etc. and/or participating in relays develop gross motor skills. Organized games involving skipping around things to music with various rhythms, and activities requiring twisting, turning, and bending all develop gross motor skills, preparing children for lifelong engagement in sports activities.

Muscles involved in fine motor movements

Fine motor movements use small muscles in the eyes, lips, tongue, wrists, fingers, and toes. Fine/small motor movements work together with gross/large muscle movements to develop movement skills and patterns. Fine motor skills are often used for purposes of functional and expressive communication, like using tools, creating artworks, and writing and typing language. Eye-hand coordination, eye-foot coordination, and manual and finger dexterity are required for the fine motor movements used in drawing, writing, and typing. Fine motor practice also develops children's tactile (touch) awareness and spatial awareness. Rolling dough/putty/clay into balls and/or hiding things inside them promote fine motor skills. Tearing and cutting paper along dotted lines and creating patterns teach accurate size and shape perception and formation. Stringing, lacing, and creating structures using plastic building blocks develop hand-eye coordination and skills needed to create color patterns. Flip cards, pegs, and stickers promote object placement skills. Writing skills are developed by writing letters/numbers in shaving cream, sand, pudding, and/or on chalkboards using wet makeup sponges/cotton swabs; using toothbrushes on dry erase boards; and practicing placement on cardboard using rice, beans, wet/dry pasta, glitter, etc.

Cooking and self-care activities

Young children are often fascinated by adults' cooking activities, want to participate, and offer to help. Involving them is not only beneficial to their self-esteem, but also develops various skills. Measuring amounts of liquids and solids in different forms develops children's math skills. Mixing, stirring, and blending ingredients using different parts of their hands develop children's fine motor skills. Life skills include self-care skills, such as combing one's hair, brushing one's teeth, fastening and unfastening buttons and snaps on clothing, and lacing and unlacing shoes. Life skills also require being able to open and close drawers, doors, and jars; to clean a house; and to wash things. It is necessary to children's normal development that they learn to combine multiple fine motor skills. Children's development of fine motor skills also needs to be integrated with the development of various self-care and other life skills (such as those described above) that are required for normal activities of daily living.

Cephalocaudal and proximodistal development

Infant and child motor development follows the same developmental sequences as prenatal embryonic and fetal physical development. Cephalocaudal means head to tail. Just as the body develops from the head down before birth, babies and young children develop motor control of their heads before they develop control of their legs. Proximodistal means near to far (i.e. central to distant). Head, torso, and arm control develop before hand and finger control. Babies learn a lot about how things look, sound, and feel once they master gross motor skills for reaching and grasping. These then evolve toward fine motor skills. For example, at around three months of age an infant's voluntary reaching gradually becomes more accurate. The infant will not need arm guidance, because he or she has spatial awareness of location and motion. Babies reach less by five months when they can move things within reach. By nine months, babies can redirect reaching to grasp objects moving in different directions. By six to twelve months, development of the pincer grasp enhances babies' capacities for object manipulation.

Benefits of physical activity

When young children engage in physical activity, they learn new motor skills and reinforce, advance, and refine existing ones. They also learn important early math skills like spatial awareness. Whenever they attempt new activities, they encounter challenges, such as having to develop higher levels of coordination, control, precision, strength, speed, flexibility, and agility. They are also challenged to coordinate their mental and physical processes more closely and in a manner that is more complex. They learn to exert effort, and to persevere in the face of difficulty. When they succeed at meeting these challenges, their self-esteem and self-efficacy (sense of competence to perform tasks) are enhanced. Since motor skills generally develop ahead of language skills, physical activity is a valuable means of direct self-expression. Young children learn many social skills through interacting with peers and adults during physical games, sports activities, etc. In addition to all these benefits, young children normally seek out physical activity, deriving a great deal of fun and enjoyment through moving, playing games/sports, and interacting physically with others.

Influences of physical, emotional, and social factors

Young children who have already become overweight/obese because of an improper diet and lack of exercise are more likely than children who are within a healthy weight range to find physical activity uncomfortable and avoid it. Even those who enjoy activity are more at risk of injury if they are overweight or lack physical conditioning. Exercise is more challenging for children with illnesses. For example, asthma interferes with breathing. Therefore, asthmatic children must be supervised and monitored when exercising. So must diabetic children, whose blood sugar can fluctuate excessively due to exercising. Their food intake must be monitored and coordinated with exercise. Children with physical disabilities may require adaptive equipment and/or alternative methods of physical instruction and exercising. Emotionally, children experiencing depression are likely to be apathetic and uninterested in movement. Hyperactive children (e.g., those with ADHD) are often overactive physically to the point of exhaustion. Children lacking adequate social skills, friends, and/or peer groups have fewer opportunities and are less likely to engage in physical games and sports with others, so their motor skills and physical fitness may suffer.

Recommendations for physical activity

The World Health Organization (WHO) advises that children between the ages of 5 and 17 should engage in a minimum of 1 hour (continuously or incrementally) of moderate to vigorous physical activity per day. According to the World Health Organization, exercising for more than one hour daily (within reason) will confer additional health benefits. The majority of children's physical activity should be aerobic in nature. Aerobic exercise uses large muscle groups, is rhythmic and continuous, and works the heart and lungs so that the pulmonary and cardiovascular systems become more efficient at absorbing and transporting oxygen. Children should take part in exercises and/or activities that strengthen the muscles and bones through weight bearing and other methods at least three times per week. Children's play activities that can fulfill bone-strengthening requirements include running, jumping, turning, and playing various games. Engaging in general play, playing games, playing sports, doing chores, using exercise as a means of transportation (e.g., walking, biking, etc.), participating in planned exercise sessions, and attending physical education classes are all activities available in family, community, and school settings that can allow children to meet physical activity and fitness requirements.

Circulatory system

The circulatory system continuously supplies blood containing oxygen and nutrients to all body tissue cells, exchanges oxygenated blood for the waste products produced during the metabolism process, and transports waste for elimination. Central to the vascular (vessel) system is the heart, which is located in the mediastinum within the thoracic cavity. The heart is encased and protected by the pericardium, a double-walled, tough fibrous sac. The heart has four chambers: two atria and two ventricles. A system of valves regulates opening/closing among the chambers, the aorta, the pulmonary artery, and the great vessels. The aorta, originating at the heart, is the body's largest artery. The pulmonary artery branches to the left and to the right, and transports venous blood from the heart's lower right chamber to the lung for oxygenation. The pulmonary veins return oxygenated blood from the lung to the left atrium of the heart. The superior and inferior venae cavae are vessels that empty into the heart's right atrium.

Integumentary and musculoskeletal systems

In the human body, the integumentary system consists of skin, hair, nails, and oil and sweat glands. The skin has three layers: the epidermis, the dermis, and subcutaneous tissues. Skin protects tissues underneath it from bacterial infections, blocks most chemicals from entering, prevents fluid loss, and reduces the probability of mechanical injury to underlying body structures. Skin regulates body temperature and synthesizes needed chemicals. It is also a sense organ, as it has sensory receptors for touch, pressure, heat/cold, and pain. It also contains motor fibers that enable necessary reactions to these sensations and stimuli. The musculoskeletal system includes bones, joints, and connective tissues: tendons, ligaments, and cartilage. It is responsible for our body shape, and provides stability and support. It also protects our internal organs and enables locomotion. Bones store calcium and other minerals, and bone marrow produces required blood cells. Muscle fibers contract to enable movement. Depending on their innervation, muscles can have voluntary or involuntary (like the heart) movements. Muscles need blood supply and oxygen to work. Thus, the musculoskeletal system depends on other systems, including the circulatory, nervous, and respiratory systems.

Lymphatic system

The lymphatic system includes lymph (a fluid), collection ducts, and tissues. Lymphatic tissues comprise the lymph nodes, the thymus gland, the tonsils, and the Peyer's patches of the intestinal tract. Lymphoid components are also present in the lungs, the mucosa in the stomach and the appendix, and the bone marrow. Microscopic capillaries merge to form lymph-collecting ducts. These ducts drain to specific centers of lymphatic tissue. The lymph system's functioning is supported by the spleen and thymus glands. While not all characteristics and functions of the lymphatic system are established, known functions include: return transportation of lymph, protein, and microorganisms to the cardiovascular system; production of lymphocytes by the lymph nodes; filtering of the blood by the lymph nodes; production of antibodies to enable immune response against infection; absorption of fats and fat soluble substances from the intestine; formation of blood cells in response to some illnesses/conditions; and phagocytosis (i.e. the surrounding/swallowing/"eating" of infectious particles by cells lining the sinuses of the lymph nodes, spleen, and liver). The lymph system defends the body against infection and supports the veins by helping to return fluids to the bloodstream.

Respiratory system

The respiratory system provides oxygen to the body and removes carbon dioxide, the waste product of respiration (breathing). In doing so, the respiratory system and many other body systems work together through complex interactions. Twelve thoracic vertebrae, twelve pairs of ribs, the sternum, the diaphragm, and the intercostal muscles comprise the thoracic cage containing the lungs. As one breathes in and out, the thoracic cage is always moving. The diaphragm, a muscular wall dividing the chest cavity and abdominal cavity, functions as a bellows for breathing. (It also plays a role in expelling feces and delivering babies.) There are air pathways between the nose/mouth, pharynx, trachea, bronchi, bronchioles, and lungs. Alveoli, tiny air sacs in the lungs, exchange oxygen and carbon dioxide. During inspiration/inhalation, the ribs and sternum rise, the diaphragm contracts and lowers, the intercostal muscles contract, air pressure in the lungs decreases, and air enters the lungs. During exhalation, the intercostal muscles and diaphragm relax, the ribs and sternum return to a resting position, air pressure in the lungs increases, and air exits the lungs.

Digestive system

The chief functions of the digestive system are to provide nutrition to the body's cells and eliminate waste products left after nourishment is extracted from foods. The process consists of three phases: ingestion (i.e. taking in foods and liquids), digestion (i.e. converting ingested nutrients through physical and chemical means into forms that the cells of the body tissues can absorb and distribute), and elimination (i.e. removing the byproducts of digestion—also known as waste—that cannot be utilized). Other body systems work with the digestive system to process nutrients. For example, the nervous system plays a role in appetite, which is a signal for us to eat. The central nervous system also stimulates the release and flow of digestive juices. The endocrine system supplies chemicals (e.g., juices from the pancreas) that aid in digestion. The circulatory system delivers digested and absorbed nutrients to the tissue cells, and also picks up waste products produced as a result of the metabolism process.

During chewing, our teeth and tongue physically break down food. Glands secrete saliva to provide lubrication during chewing and swallowing, and provide digestive enzymes to begin the process of chemically breaking down the foods we eat. The pharynx delivers food to the esophagus, where muscular contractions (peristalsis) move food downward. The epiglottis closes the trachea (windpipe) during swallowing to prevent food from being aspirated into the lungs. Glands in the stomach lining secrete gastric fluid comprised of hydrochloric acid and other chemicals, which dissolve food into semiliquid chyme. Chyme gradually passes into the small intestine, where most digestion and absorption occur. The small intestine is made up of the duodenum, the jejunum, and the ileum. The pancreas secretes digestive juices, the gallbladder secretes bile, and the intestinal mucosa secretes other juices into the duodenum to digest chyme. Digested nutrients are absorbed through the intestinal walls into capillaries and lymphatic vessels to be distributed to body cells. The large intestine consists of the cecum, the colon (ascending, transverse, descending, and sigmoid), the rectum, and the anus. The colon completes digestion and absorption, and delivers wastes to the rectum, which eliminates them through the anus.

Central nervous system

Some main functions of the central nervous system (i.e. the brain and spinal cord) include controlling consciousness and all mental processes, regulating the functions and movements of the body, and sending and receiving nerve impulses to and from all parts of the body. For example, when we touch something hot, sensory nerve endings in our fingers send impulses to the brain, which interprets them as heat and sends a signal along motor nerves to pull our fingers away. The autonomic nervous system is automatic and involuntary. For example, it makes our heart beat. We cannot voluntarily start/stop our heartbeat. The voluntary nervous system is under our conscious control. For example, our brains use it to send impulses to our skeletal muscles when we want to sit/stand/walk, etc., which contract in response. The autonomic nervous system is divided into parasympathetic and sympathetic components. The parasympathetic portion stimulates muscular activity in the organs and gland secretion. The sympathetic portion stimulates heartbeat, vasoconstriction, and sweating. These two portions of the autonomic nervous system oppose/balance each other to regulate system

Urinary system

The function of the urinary system is to eliminate the liquid wastes produced through nutrient metabolism by excreting them from the body. The urinary system is made up of two kidneys, two ureters, the bladder, and the urethra. Behind the abdominal cavity at the thoraco-lumbar level are the kidneys, a pair of large bean-shaped glands. They continually remove water, salts, toxins, and nitrogenous wastes from the bloodstream, and convert these substances into urine. Urine droplets flow from the kidneys into the ureters. The ureters are long, narrow tubes carrying urine to the bladder, which is a hollow, muscular, elastic organ. When enough urine collects in the bladder, nerves stimulate the body to empty it via urination. In human females, the urethra is about an inch and a half long, and is located in the upper vaginal wall. In males, the urethra is about eight inches long, and extends from the bladder through the prostate gland and the penis. Both urine and sperm pass through the male urethra, while the female urethra and vaginal canal are separate.

Endocrine system

The human endocrine system is one of the most complex body systems. Scientists understand many of its functions, but not all of them. It is a system of ductless, internally secreting glands (some necessary to life) that extract various substances from tissue fluids and the bloodstream to create completely new substances (i.e. hormones). Operating without ducts, endocrine glands secrete hormones directly into the blood and lymph circulatory systems for distribution to the organs. The endocrine system's main glands include the pituitary, thyroid, parathyroid, and adrenal glands; the Islets of Langerhans in the pancreas; and the gonads (male testes and female ovaries). Additionally, the pancreas is both an endocrine and an exocrine gland. Its endocrine (internal secretion) function is to secrete insulin to regulate sugar metabolism; its exocrine (external secretion) function is to secrete pancreatic juice into the duodenum to aid in digestion. If the pancreas produces insufficient insulin, type 1 diabetes results. If the body responds insufficiently to insulin, type 2 diabetes results.

Pituitary, thyroid, and parathyroid glands

The pituitary and thyroid glands are both components of the endocrine system. The pituitary gland functions directly by regulating physical growth, development, and sexual maturation in children and adolescents; regulating the retention and excretion of fluid; regulating the balance of electrolytes (sodium, potassium, and chloride) in blood and tissues; and regulating new mothers' lactation (milk production). The pituitary is termed the hypophyseal /"master gland" because it also regulates all other glands in the endocrine system. Therefore, it is involved in regulating food assimilation and metabolism through hydrating the thyroid gland; regulating body composition, adaptation, and resistance to stress through acting on the adrenal and parathyroid glands; regulating breathing, circulation, digestion, urine excretion, and muscular action through the collective activity of multiple hormones; and regulating sexual development, activity, and reproduction through acting on the gonads. The thyroid gland manufactures and secretes hormones that regulate child growth and development, as well as certain metabolic processes and their rates. It also stores iodine. The parathyroid glands secrete hormones that regulate blood calcium levels, phosphorus metabolism, and muscle and nervous system excitation.

Reproductive system

The external female reproductive organs include the mons pubis, the labia majora, the labia minora, the clitoris, the vestibule, the hymen, the Bartholin's glands, and several other glands. The breasts/mammary glands can also be considered parts of the reproductive system, as they produce milk for infants following reproduction. Internal organs include the vagina, the two fallopian tubes, the uterus, and the two ovaries. Hormones stimulate either ovary to produce an ovum/egg roughly once a month. A follicle containing an egg cell forms. When the egg matures, the follicle ruptures, releasing the egg. This is known as ovulation. The ovum passes into a fallopian tube and travels toward the uterus. Hormones have meanwhile also stimulated the endometrium (uterine lining) to thicken and increase its blood supply. When the egg reaches the womb, it is implanted in the endometrium if it was fertilized in the fallopian tube by a male sperm. This is known as conception. If the egg was not fertilized, hormone signals subside, causing the endometrium to detach from the uterine wall. The sloughed off endometrial tissue, the resulting blood, and the unfertilized egg exit the body. This process is known as menstruation.

The scrotum and the penis are the external reproductive organs of the human male. The internal organs of the male reproductive system include two testes, two epididymides, two seminal ducts, two seminal vesicles, two ejaculatory ducts, two spermatic cords, the urethra, the prostate gland, and several other glands. The testes, which are glandular organs, hang on either side of the scrotum from spermatic cords. These cords contain the vas deferens, blood vessels, and supportive tissues. Male sperm cells and hormones are produced by the testes. Each testis has an epididymis connecting it to the vas deferens, an excretory seminal duct. The vas deferens travel upward inside the spermatic cords to the prostate gland, which is in front of the neck of the urinary bladder. There, the vas deferens join with the pouch-like glands called seminal vesicles to form ejaculatory ducts. The prostate gland and seminal vesicles secrete substances into the semen that promote sperm motility. The ejaculatory ducts release semen into the urethra, and from here the semen is ejected through the penis during sexual intercourse.

Human brain

The brain is divided into five major parts: the cerebrum, the midbrain, the cerebellum, the pons, and the medulla oblongata. The cranial nerves are: I – olfactory, which controls the sense of smell; II – optic, which controls vision; III – oculomotor, which controls the movements of the eye muscles, the movements of the upper eyelids, and the pupillary reflexes (expanding and contracting to admit more/less light); IV – trochlear, which controls the movements of the superior oblique eye muscles; V – trigeminal, which controls facial sensation, the eye's corneal reflex, and chewing; VI – abducens, which controls the movements of the lateral rectus eye muscle; VII –

facial, which controls movement of the facial muscles and the taste sensation in the front two-thirds of the tongue; VIII – vestibulocochlear, which controls equilibrium (balance) via the vestibular system in the inner ear, and hearing (the cochlea is in the inner ear); IX – glossopharyngeal, which controls the taste sensation in the rear one-third of the tongue; X – vagus, which controls pharyngeal contraction (gag reflex), vocal cord movements, and soft palate movements; XI – spinal accessory, which controls movement of the sternocleidomastoid and trapezius muscles; and XII – hypoglossal, which controls tongue movements.

National standards regarding the knowledge and abilities related to physical education

The National Association for Sport and Physical Education (NASPE) has developed six national physical education standards. These standards state that someone who is physically educated: (1) shows the motor skills and patterns of movement competencies s/he needs to conduct various physical activities; (2) shows comprehension of the basic concepts, main principles, methods, and techniques of movement as they relate to learning and executing physical activities; (3) regularly engages in physical activity; (4) reaches and sustains a level of physical fitness that enhances health; (5) demonstrates behaviors, personally and socially, that reflect self-respect and respect for others within contexts of physical activity; and (6) places value upon the benefits of physical activities and of being fit and active, such as the pleasure; the improvement and maintenance of health; the physical, personal, and social challenges; and the opportunities to interact socially and express oneself.

The Arts

Main functions of art

Artworks can be created for physical, social, and personal purposes. When art focuses on the social lives of groups rather than on one individual's experiences or viewpoint, it serves social functions. Art carrying political stances/messages always performs social functions. Dadaist Oppenheim's hair-covered tea set did not perform any physical function, but served social functions by politically protesting World War I and many other social/political issues. During the Great Depression, photographers like Dorothea Lange, Gordon Parks, Walker Evans, and Arthur Rothstein commissioned by the Farm Security Administration produced stark records of people's suffering. These depictions of social conditions also served social functions. Fine artists like Francisco Goya and William Hogarth, as well as cartoonists like Thomas Nast and Charles Bragg, created satirical works of art lampooning various social and political customs and situations. Satire is intended not only to provide comic relief, insight, and perspective, but also to stimulate social change. Therefore, it serves social functions. Another social function is improving community status and pride through art treasures.

Works of art can have physical, social, and personal functions. Of these three, the personal functions of art are the most variable. Artists' motivations to create works include the desire to express their feelings and ideas, to obtain gratification through producing art, to communicate messages to viewers, to enable both themselves and their viewers to have an aesthetic experience, and to simply entertain viewers. Some artists also claim that they sometimes create art for no particular reason, and that the art produced has no meaning. Art can perform a personal function of control. For example, some artists use their work to give order to the world's apparent chaos. Others use art to create chaos in an overly orderly, boring environment. Art can be therapeutic for both artists and viewers. Much art has served the personal function of religion. Artworks with biological purposes, like cultural fertility symbols or bodily decorations designed to attract mates for procreation, are also examples of the personal functions of art.

Determining the functions of art
Ascertaining the function of a work of art requires considering its context. Half of the context involves the artist. Knowing the artist's country, the historical time period during which the artist lived, and the social and political culture of the time informs artwork and our ability to infer what the artist was thinking and intending when he or she was creating it. The other half of the context involves the viewer. Knowing what the artwork means to you in your own place and time informs your perception of and response to it. Taken within context, art serves physical, personal, and social functions. For example, architecture, industrial design, and crafts have physical functions. A raku pottery bowl made in Japan serves a physical function during a tea ceremony. However, a teacup covered with hair (paired with a hair-covered saucer and spoon) by Dada artist Meret Oppenheim (1936) makes an artistic statement, but serves no physical function. When we view a tribal war club in a museum, regardless of the exquisite craftsmanship it may demonstrate, we realize it was made primarily for bludgeoning enemies.

Learning outcomes

The arts are just as important to include in curricula as language, math, science, social studies, health, and physical education. Early learning standards in many states now reflect the goal to integrate the arts into the overall curriculum. Teachers need to provide young children with activities that promote development of fine motor skills, exploration of art materials and processes, and symbolic representation of concepts through artworks. EC educators should not merely assign isolated art activities. They can clarify many concepts and improve learning by providing art projects that fit into the overall curriculum and are relevant to individual learning units. Teachers should develop detailed, well-organized step lists for each activity. Clear directions not only maintain classroom order, but also provide children with a structure within which to experiment with art and enhance their sequencing skills. Teachers should use process-oriented activities, both on their own and within lessons that require products. For example, painting pictures of animals combines product (representing an animal) with process (exploring paint use). Teachers should supply and explain rules/steps for process activities that explore the use of art materials and processes.

Learning objectives

When children participate in teacher-designed art activities, they can fulfill learning objectives such as exploring various art materials and processes; developing awareness of visual art and its basic elements (e.g., line, shape, color, and texture); using art forms to represent feelings, thoughts, and/or stories; developing the skills of color recognition and discrimination; and even building their vocabularies and language skills, depending on the activities. Teachers can integrate such objectives with an overall theme for each art activity/project that they integrate with the current theme for their lesson or curriculum unit. For example, if space travel is the class theme one week, constructing model rocket ships is more appropriate than painting self-portraits. Even open-ended activities to explore art materials and processes can be integrated with thematic units. For example, teachers can apply activities exploring cutting and gluing processes to a theme of one specific color by providing various materials and textures that are all the same color. In this way, teachers can connect a learning concept to experimentation with artistic processes.

Planning an art activity or project

EC teachers should first establish the concept they want to teach, the objectives they want to meet through planning and teaching the lesson/activity, and the learning objectives they want the children to meet through participating. Then, a teacher can construct a simple prototype for the project. This enables the teacher to estimate how long it will take the children to complete the activity, and to explore and discover the optimal sequencing of steps for the activity. The teacher should then write down the plan, step-by-step. Steps should include those that need to be completed before the activity. These might include preliminary discussion, book reading/sharing related to the project, viewing related artworks and/or photos, etc. Steps should also include those that need to be completed while setting up the activity, such as dispensing paints, clay, etc.; assembling paintbrushes/other instruments; and passing out paper and other materials. Teachers do not need to be artistically proficient. Young children are not art critics, and teachers can find a great deal of information about art materials and processes by reading books and searching online. Available professional development courses focusing on art can also give teachers more ideas for lesson plans.

Production and reception of works of art

In all branches of the arts, artists and their audiences (who may also be participants in the case of performance art) complete three basic artistic processes that are closely related: creation, performance, and response. The performance process includes five steps. (1) <u>Selecting</u> is the step during which the artist makes a choice about what to present. For example, musicians choose pieces to play. Dancers choose choreographic pieces to perform. Visual artists select which of their paintings, drawings, sculptures, mobiles/stabiles etc. to display. Theater producers, directors, and actors choose a play to perform. (2) <u>Analyzing</u> is the step during which the performer researches the background of the chosen work and analyzes its structure to understand it and its import. (3) <u>Interpreting</u> is the step during which the performer develops a personal idea about what the work should express or accomplish. (4) <u>Rehearsing, evaluating, and refining</u> is the step during which the performer applies her/his skills and techniques to develop a personal interpretation that will enable her/his performance to make the work come alive. The artist then evaluates the performance, and makes further refinements to subsequent presentations. (5) <u>Presenting</u> is the final step, during which the artist performs the work for others.

Three processes common to all branches of the arts—visual, musical, dance, dramatic, and performance art—are creating, performing, and responding. The first of these, creating, involves the genesis of the artistic product. There are several steps in creating. (1) <u>Imagining</u> is the step during which the artist develops his/her ideas and considers the concepts and feelings which s/he wants to communicate and express through the work. (2) <u>Planning</u> is the step during which the artist researches, experiments with, and designs the means by which s/he will present her/his ideas and emotions (e.g., the materials that will be used and how they will be manipulated to produce the desired effects). (3) <u>Making, evaluating, and refining</u> is the step during which the artist applies her/his skills and various techniques to create an artistic product that will bring her/his ideas and feelings to life. (4) <u>Presenting</u> is the step during which the artist exhibits visual art in a gallery, private exhibit, or another type of showing. The artist might also perform music, dance, theater, or performance art for an audience so that others can participate in and respond to the artwork.

Fundamental artistic processes

Works of art, whether visual, musical, dramatic, literary, dance, or performance art, all involve three basic and interrelated processes: creation of the work, performance of the work for others, and the response of others (e.g., audiences, participants, viewers, or readers). The artistic process of responding to artwork includes four steps. (1) <u>Selection</u> is the step during which the person(s) who will receive the artwork choose what they want to experience (possible choices include attending a gallery exhibit of paintings, drawings, or sculptures; going to see a theatrical play or a movie; attending a dance performance; attending/participating in a performance art show; or reading a book of poetry or prose). (2) <u>Analysis</u> is the step during which the viewers/audience/participants/readers see/hear and understand the components of the work, and mentally bring these components together to perceive the work as a whole. (3) <u>Interpretation</u> is the step during which those experiencing the work and/or its performance construct meaning from what they have witnessed, developing a personal response to the creator(s)' and performer(s)' expressions of concepts and emotions. (4) <u>Evaluation</u> is the final step, during which the respondent(s) assess the quality of the artwork and of its performance.

Artistic processes facilitate learning

The artistic processes have many steps in common. This interrelatedness among the processes informs students' development of educated responses to artworks. For instance, when students learn the step of evaluating their own artworks, they learn to apply better critical approaches when interpreting the artworks created by others. They also use their experiences to direct their selection of works they want to witness and respond to in the future. When students learn how to evaluate and refine their own work, this facilitates their subsequent evaluation and selection of others' works to watch, to perform themselves, and/or to purchase. Teachers can promote this by encouraging students to transfer their learning from one artistic process to another. For example, teachers can introduce students to others' work while they are creating their own so they can transfer what they learn about the creation process to the responding process. When students are solving specific creative/artistic problems, teachers can expose them to other artists' solutions and encourage students to consider these solutions.

Line

In visual media, a line is the path of a moving point; the edge of a flat or two-dimensional shape; or the outline of a solid, three-dimensional object. Lines are longer than they are wide. The term measure refers to the width of a line. Lines can be straight, curved, wavy, angular, or zigzag. Lines can be horizontal (side to side), vertical (up and down), or diagonal (at an angle between vertical and horizontal). Lines can also be implied. In this case, they are not physically present, but the artist's arrangement of other elements suggests lines, which organize the picture and/or guide viewers' eyes. The movement a line follows/appears to show is called direction. Where and how a line is placed in a picture/design is called location. Lines define areas, and imply or create open or closed shapes like circles, rectangles, etc. Line combined with shape creates implied volume in paintings/drawings and actual volume in sculptures. Lines express various qualities by being jagged, loopy, bold, repetitive, etc., and evoke different emotional and mental viewer responses.

Shape, form, and value

Shape refers to two-dimensional areas created by connecting lines to outline the contours of objects depicted in art. Shapes can be positive or negative (i.e. defined not by their own outlines, but by the edges of surrounding shapes). Shapes may be biomorphic (i.e. shapes found in nature) or geometric. Variations in value, texture, or color can make shapes stand out in a piece. Form is the three-dimensional projection of shape. Form has dimension and volume. In paintings and drawings, form appears to have mass, while in sculptures it actually does have mass. The term "form" can also be used to describe an artwork's overall structure. Value refers to the appearance and range of lights and darks seen in a visual work of art. Regardless of color, value varies between black and white, with an indefinite range of various shades of gray between these two absolutes.

Texture and space

Texture refers to how rough or smooth a surface appears and/or feels. Everyday materials have texture, as do works of art. An object or a work of art can look and/or feel spongy or glassy, wet or dry, soft or hard, etc. Texture can be real, as with sandpaper and other rough-textured materials used to create works of art. Or, it can be illusory, as when materials appear hard or soft, but are really not. Space is defined as the measurable distance between predetermined points. It can be shallow or limited, with a foreground and a background; or it can be deep or extended, with a middle ground as well as a foreground and a background. Two-dimensional space has height and width; three-dimensional space has height and width, plus volume and time. Like negative shape (shape that is not defined by its own outlines, but by the surrounding shapes and their outlines), negative space appears in art. It is the space around and between the positive objects or shapes depicted. This negative space forms its own shapes around positive subjects.

Rhythm

In visual art, rhythm is achieved through repeating visual movement. Visual movement is created by arranging lines, shapes, and/or colors to give the viewer's eye a sense of motion and direction. Just as we hear rhythm in music through aural beats and varying note durations, we see rhythm in paintings through visual movement of lines, angles, shapes, and other elements. Just as Beethoven used repetition of musical phrases and themes to create mood, drama, and movement, artists use movement and repetition to create visual rhythm. For example, in "Nude Descending a Staircase, No. 2" (1912) by Marcel Duchamp, the artist depicts an abstracted human figure, repeating the figure using overlapping placements in a diagonal, downward pattern. The series of repeated shapes and angles gives the impression of viewing action in strobe lighting or via stop action photography. The figures are physically still, but visually convey the effect of moving down a staircase. By directionally repeating the figure, Duchamp shows movement and rhythm within the static medium of a painting.

Color

Color refers to the wavelengths of light reflected by a surface. Some wavelengths are absorbed by paints and other visual art media/materials; we do not see these. Other wavelengths are reflected; these are the ones we see as colors. Primary colors are pure, individual colors that cannot be separated into other colors or produced by mixing colors. The three primary colors are red, blue, and yellow. Secondary colors are combinations of two primary colors (e.g., orange = red + yellow, green = blue + yellow, and purple/violet = red + blue). Intermediate colors are produced by mixing a primary and a secondary color (e.g., red-orange, yellow-orange, blue-green, yellow-green, blue-violet, or red-violet). Colors are arranged on the color wheel. Analogous colors are adjacent to each other on the wheel. Examples of analogous colors include yellow and orange, orange and red, blue and green, and green and yellow. Complementary colors are opposite each other on the color wheel. Examples of complementary colors include blue and orange, yellow and purple, and red and green. Mixing equal parts of two complementary colors produces brown. Blue and predominantly blue colors are cool. Red, yellow, and predominantly red/yellow colors are warm. Colors identify objects, evoke moods, and influence emotions.

Balance

Balance refers to how visual weight is distributed in a work of visual art. In two-dimensional art like paintings, balance is the visual equilibrium among the painting's elements, which make the entire picture look balanced. Balance can be symmetrical (both sides are equal) or asymmetrical, with shapes and spaces that are unequal and/or unevenly distributed. This produces psychological rather than physical balance, creating tension and suggesting movement. Radial balance/symmetry uses images radiating from a center, such as wheel spokes or ripples around a pebble thrown into water. An example of balance is seen in the painting "Dressing for the Carnival" (1877) by Winslow Homer. The central figure of a carnival performer putting on his costume is the focal point. The performer is surrounded by two adult assistants and a group of fascinated children who are watching him. The shapes, values, and colors are balanced to produce overall visual equilibrium and unity (another organizing principle of art).

Pattern

Pattern is the organized or random repetition of elements. Music is made up of sound patterns. Visual patterns often appear in nature. Artists frequently create works featuring repeated designs that produce patterns inspired by those seen in the natural world. Visual art is enhanced by pattern, which enriches surface interest to augment visual excitement. For example, in "Numbers in Color" (1958-59), the artist Jasper Johns created a regular pattern by assembling 11 rows of 11 stacked rectangles each. He painted various numerical digits from 0 to 9 within most of the rectangles. He made these numbers look irregular by irregularly distributing, varying, and applying the colors he used. Many patterned paintings do not include a focal point or area. This often makes them look more like designs—even when they include recognizable images—than portraits, landscapes, still-lifes, or other types of paintings that do not have such repetitive patterning.

Visual movement

Artists create a visual sense of movement in paintings to direct the viewer's eyes. Direction is frequently toward a focal point or area within the painting. Artists can direct movement along lines, edges, shapes, and colors, but especially along parts with equal value (dark/light), which best facilitates the eyes' movement. For example, in "Liberation of the Peon" (1931), Diego Rivera depicts soldiers liberating a slave by cutting the ropes binding him while clothing his nakedness with a blanket or garment. Paths of movement in the painting all lead to the focal point of the knife cutting the ropes. (Emphasis, another art/design principle, is also seen in how the action of freeing the peon is made more important than the soldiers performing that action.) By painting all humans in the scene with their eyes focused on the slave, Rivera creates movement directing our view toward him. At the same time, he painted all horses with their eyes focused out at the viewer, drawing the viewer into the scene.

Emphasis

Artists use the design principle of emphasis to call attention to particular elements in their works. Emphasis directs the viewer's focus to certain parts of a painting, and makes certain components of a work dominant. Emphasis can be achieved in art by emphasizing various design elements like value (light/dark), color, shape, line, etc. Artists also use contrast (e.g., contrasting values, colors, shapes, etc.) to create emphasis. To emphasize a focal area, a center of interest which focuses on the most important part of a painting, an artist can create visual emphasis through extreme contrasts of light and dark values. Strongly contrasting shapes and/or marked contrasts in other design elements also create visual emphasis. As an example of visual emphasis, in the painting "At the Moulin Rouge" (1892/1895), Henri de Toulouse-Lautrec emphasizes the focal area of a group of friends conversing in a cabaret through contrasting colors and values, as well as through movement directing the eye toward the group. His use of color, light, and shape also help create the scene's atmosphere.

Unity

One of the most important characteristics of a well-developed work of visual art is its visual unity. When we view a painting without unity, we may see a collection of disconnected parts that do not come together to form a whole. We may perceive it as fragmentary, disorganized, and incomplete. When an artist achieves visual unity, all of the elements in a painting appear to belong together. Unity affords paintings the quality of cohesion that makes them look and feel finished and complete. For example, in the painting "Starry Night" (1889), Vincent Van Gogh used his characteristic large, visible brush strokes in a swirly pattern throughout the landscape, providing visual unity through the texture, rhythm, pattern, and movement of the lines and shapes. He used predominantly cool colors (blues and bluish browns), providing unity through color. (He also provided emphasis by adding contrasting yellow stars.) The result is a unified painting whose elements work together, strongly conveying the atmosphere, mood, emotion, and story that the artist wanted to express.

Contrast

Contrast refers to significant differences in the values (lights and darks), colors, textures, shapes, lines, and other elements of visual artworks. Visual contrast creates interest and excitement, and avoids monotony in art. For example, in the painting "Still Life with Apples and Peaches" (1905), Paul Cézanne combined all seven elements and all seven principles of design to create a unified composition. Among these, he used at least eight kinds of contrast: (1) unpatterned vs. intricately patterned surfaces (pattern contrast); (2) soft vs. hard/found edges (edge contrast); (3) dark vs. light vs. middle values (value contrast); (4) pure vs. muted/blended colors (intensity contrast); (5) cool vs. warm colors (temperature contrast); (6) textured vs. smooth surfaces (texture contrast); (7) organic vs. geometric shapes (shape contrast); and (8) large vs. small objects/shapes (size contrast).

Pitch, tempo, and rhythm

Pitch is the frequency of a sound, such as a musical note. We hear high/middle/low frequency sound waves as high/middle/low pitched sounds. Various pitches are combined in musical compositions to create variety. A series of connected notes of different pitches creates a melody. Sounding (playing/singing) several pitches simultaneously and combining them produces harmonies and chords. Connected series of harmonies/chords in turn create harmonic/chord progressions. Tempo is the speed of music. Fast tempo can evoke happiness, excitement, fear, anger, or urgency. Slow tempo can evoke serenity, grandeur, solemnity, sadness, or ominousness. Musical compositions commonly direct the tempo using terms like andante (walking speed), adagio (slow), allegro (happy/quick), lento (slow), largo (expansively slow), etc. Rhythm includes the overall beat/time signature (number of beats per measure) and the variations among note lengths that produce patterns (e.g., legato describes smoothly connected series of notes, while staccato describes sharply disconnected notes that are cut short and sounded separately). Composers combine pitch, tempo, and rhythm in music to create atmosphere and mood, and to evoke emotion in listeners. They also arrange these elements to construct/recall musical themes/motifs within compositions.

Practice Test

Reading and English Language Arts

1. Children develop phonological awareness:
    a. Only through direct training given by adults.
    b. Only naturally, through exposure to language.
    c. Via both natural exposure and direct training.
    d. Via neither incidental exposure nor instruction.

2. In early childhood, phonological awareness skills typically develop:
    a. Gradually.
    b. Suddenly.
    c. In no order.
    d. In school.

3. Young children's skills in phonological awareness are focused on:
    a. Morphologies.
    b. Speech sounds.
    c. Word meanings.
    d. Word sequence.

4. A young child with normally developing phonological awareness, when listening to spoken language, should be able to identify:
    a. Assonance.
    b. Consonance.
    c. Alliteration.
    d. All of these.

5. Which of the following has research found most predictive of children's future long-term literacy performance?
    a. Their scores on standardized intelligence tests
    b. Their family's relative socioeconomic status
    c. Their phonological and phonemic awareness
    d. Their early knowledge of vocabulary words

6. What statement is accurate regarding normally developing oral language in children?
    a. There is a considerable range of ages within normal individual growth.
    b. There are no individual differences among developmental milestones.
    c. Individual children achieve oral language milestones at specified ages.
    d. Individual children all develop spoken language skills at the same rates.

7. To support EC language development, experts advise which of the following teacher practices?
    a. Asking children linear or one-way questions
    b. Doing most of the talking in their classrooms
    C. Focusing on durations of verbal interactions
    D. Asking children more open-ended questions

8. A student learning English as a second language (ESL) who has limited comprehension of English and can speak one- to two-word English answers, essential English words, present-tense English verbs, and some familiar English phrases is in which stage of second-language acquisition?
   a. Preproduction
   b. Early Production
   c. Speech Emergence
   d. Intermediate Fluency

9. A child who omits, substitutes, or distorts certain speech sounds beyond the usual age-range norms is most likely to have:
   a. An articulation disorder.
   b. A type of voice disorder.
   c. One specific type of aphasia.
   d. Delayed language development.

10. A four-year-old child who does not correctly or clearly produce the speech sounds /r/ and /s/:
    a. Likely has delayed language development.
    b. Likely has normal articulatory development.
    c. Likely has some degree of hearing impairment.
    d. Likely needs early intervention for stuttering.

11. The Alphabetic Principle is *best* defined as the concept that:
    a. The letters of the alphabet are arranged in a specific sequence.
    b. The letters of the alphabet are combined to spell various words.
    c. The letters of the alphabet represent corresponding phonemes.
    d. The letters of the alphabet are used to create matching sounds.

12. Which is true about instruction to improve preschoolers' alphabetic knowledge as needed?
    a. Teachers should give only explicit instruction in isolated letter-sound matches.
    b. Teachers should only integrate letter-sound correspondences into curriculum.
    c. Teachers should provide opportunities for practice, but not isolated instruction.
    d. Teachers should combine explicit instruction, integration, and ways to practice.

13. What is true about teaching ESL students English-language reading, including alphabetic knowledge?
    a. Formal instruction in a second language can accelerate students' acquisition of English.
    b. Teachers should require ESL students to master each curriculum element consecutively.
    c. Providing students with linguistic activities meaningful to them promotes ESL acquisition.
    d. Letter-to-sound correspondences are the same across languages, so they transfer easily.

14. Which of these is accurate regarding young children's development of print awareness?
    a. The most common age for children to develop print awareness is between five and seven years.
    b. Research finds that four-year-olds are likely to acquire print concepts before word concepts.
    c. Preschoolers who attain print literacy skills are no more likely to read better at later ages.
    d. Print awareness is knowing that print has meaning, but not necessarily its form/function.

15. The Interactive Book Reading teaching method promotes early literacy development and reading comprehension by incorporating all EXCEPT which of these strategies?
    a. Curriculum-embedded assessments
    b. The 3S strategy (See, Show, and Say)
    c. Asking the students "Wh-" questions
    d. The Expanded Book Reading strategy

16. Which of the following is true about the 3N (Notice, Nudge, Narrate) instructional strategy for developing early childhood literacy?
    a. It does not incorporate any informal assessment of literacy levels.
    b. It uses scaffolding to promote further literacy skills development.
    c. It is a strategy that does not integrate any reflective components.
    d. This strategy is not found adaptable to games for young children.

17. Which of the following reading comprehension strategies is *most* applicable to differentiating between homonyms without knowing their exact spellings?
    a. Pictures
    b. Phonics
    c. Context
    d. Grammar

18. Which of these is an example of attributes to seek in good children's literature?
    a. Stable story characters who do not change
    b. Books featuring overtly moralistic themes
    c. Concise summaries of race/gender types
    d. Original yet believable plot constructions

19. Which genre of children's literature is most likely to begin "Once upon a time…" and conclude with a happy ending?
    a. Modern fantasy
    b. Picture books
    c. Traditional
    d. Poetry books

20. Which of these is true regarding early signs of reading difficulties in young children?
    a. A child's inability to form rhymes is not a concern, as long as s/he can identify rhymes.
    b. A child's inability to separate words into individual phonemes can indicate a problem.
    c. A child's inability to blend individual phonemes to form words is not a sign of trouble.
    d. A child's inability to count word syllables or spell new words phonetically is immaterial.

21. Which of the following is accurate regarding conversational vs. academic English for ESL students?
    a. Conversational English is not as cognitively demanding of ESLs as academic English.
    b. Conversational English deficits are the causes for ESL academic underachievement.
    c. Conversational English is harder for ESL students to develop than academic English.
    d. Conversational English takes the same time for ESLs to develop as academic English.

22. Of the following activities that promote building vocabulary for young children, which one is *most* dependent on the teacher?
    a. Repeatedly singing the same familiar song over and over
    b. Reciting the same familiar rhymes and chants repeatedly
    c. Listening to repeated readings of the same favorite story
    d. A word wall in the classroom to illustrate words/concepts

23. Which of the following is true regarding children's reading fluency?
    a. The lack of reading fluency is always due to word-decoding deficits.
    b. Children's motivation to read is unaffected by their reading fluency.
    c. Some children need only more reading practice to develop fluency.
    d. Fluency has equal impact on school performance at all grade levels.

24. Which of these is an indication that a child has problems with reading comprehension?
    a. The child wonders about why the characters in a story did some things.
    b. The child can tell how a story s/he read ended, but cannot explain why.
    c. The child makes predictions about what will happen next in a narrative.
    d. The child associates things in the reading with things in his/her own life.

25. Regarding student problems that teachers may observe which can indicate dyslexia, which is true?
    a. Dyslexic students perform worse on objective tests than their IQ and knowledge.
    b. Students with dyslexia typically have more trouble reading long than short words.
    c. Students who have dyslexia lack fluidity, but fare much better with rote memory.
    d. Dyslexic students have equal trouble understanding words in isolation or context.

26. Concerning spelling, what statement is correct about how children learn?
    a. Children must be taught spelling patterns as they will not learn them incidentally.
    b. Children who know basic spelling rules can deduce spellings for words they hear.
    c. Children may be able to spell words, but this does not mean they can read them.
    d. Children's reading and writing skills promote spelling, but the reverse is not true.

27. According to linguists, what do invented spellings by young children best signify?
    a. Children who invent spellings lack phonemic and phonetic awareness.
    b. Children's selections of phonetic spellings are due to adult influences.
    c. Inventing spellings for words is evidence of phonetic comprehension.
    d. Diverse children choosing the same phonetic spellings is just chance.

28. In which stage of writing development do children understand that written forms symbolize meanings?
    a. Scribbling and drawing
    b. Letters
    c. Letters and spaces
    d. Letter-like forms and shapes

29. According to literacy experts, what is true about student writing for various purposes and audiences?
    a. The primary purpose of student writing is expressing their ideas, thoughts, and emotions.
    b. The primary purpose of student writing is persuading their readers to agree/believe them.
    c. Improving student reading skills improves their writing skills, but not the other way around.
    d. Improving student writing skills as well as their reading skills improves their learning ability.

30. In the POWER instructional strategy for teaching students the writing process, the P stands for:
    a. Purpose
    b. Program
    c. Planning
    d. Partners

31. One simple rating scale for assessing young children's early writing (Clay, 1993) divides skills into three areas: Language Level, Message Quality, and Directional Principles. Which of the following achievements falls into the Message Quality category?
    a. The child can write two related sentences with punctuation.
    b. The child attempts to set down his/her own ideas in writing.
    c. The child can write a story with paragraphs and two themes.
    d. The child writes showing correct spacing between the words.

32. Which of these correctly shows the normal developmental sequence of children's writing with regard to directional principles?
    a. No knowledge; partial knowledge; reverses the direction; correct direction; correct spacing
    b. No knowledge; reverses the direction; partial knowledge; correct spacing; correct direction
    c. No knowledge; partial knowledge; correct spacing; reverses the direction; correct direction
    d. No knowledge; reverses the direction; correct direction; correct spacing; partial knowledge

33. Regarding the standard conventions for written English when evaluating student writing, which of the following reflects the function of writing rather than its form?
    a. The length of the student's composition
    b. Appropriate content in the composition
    c. Word usage in a student's composition
    d. The spelling in a student's composition

34. Of the following writing examples, which one reflects an error in grammar?
    a. "She is without a doubt the very best freind I have ever had in my life."
    b. "He said we should wait two hours, we waited two hours and returned."
    c. "A great animal lover, his pets included dogs, cats, horses, and chickens."
    d. "They were traveling South at first, but later in the trip they went West."

35. Which of the following is most accurate about teacher strategies to promote young children's motivation to write?
    a. Children's enthusiasm is sustained by sticking with the same writing activities.
    b. Children are less motivated to write about subjects that are familiar to them.
    c. Children display greater writing motivation with predictable, routine activities.
    d. Children are more motivated to participate in activities that they find exciting.

36. According to research, which area of conditions motivating students to write depends critically on how the teacher conceives of writing?
    a. Cultivating student beliefs about the functionality of writing
    b. Providing authentic writing activities promoting engagement
    c. Establishing a positive emotional environment for students
    d. All of these areas rely equally on the teacher's perceptions

Mathematics

37. Regarding the relationship of cognitive problem-solving skills to mathematics, which of these is true?
    a. Problem-solving skills inform mathematical thinking but not social skills.
    b. Developing problem-solving skills aids math rather than language skills.
    c. Students apply logical reasoning to solve every day and novel problems.
    d. Children must be taught to have interest in solving everyday problems.

38. Which of the following correctly describes a characteristic of students with effective problem-solving skills?
    a. Students develop hypotheses via repeated trial-and-error tests.
    b. Students have developed demonstrated skills for self-regulation.
    c. Students are cautious in solving problems and avoid taking a risk.
    d. Students quickly switch to another problem if their solution fails.

39. Which of these is correct about mental math games adults can initiate with young children to promote their problem-solving skills for learning math?
    a. Adults should always use concrete objects within oral story problems.
    b. Adults should plan mental math games to adhere to child grade levels.
    c. Adults should always keep problems simple with only whole numbers.
    d. Adults should always tell young children correct answers to questions.

40. To support children's development of reasoning skills for comprehending and applying early math and science concepts, which of these is the best adult behavior?
 a. Asking children "why?" questions and waiting until they find the expected answers
 b. Asking children "why?" questions and disregarding both expected and real answers
 c. Asking children "why?" questions and requiring them to answer them immediately
 d. Asking children "why?" questions, giving time to think, and listening to the answers

41. Which of these is true about children's transition from intuitive thinking to formal math education?
 a. Children do not use mathematical thinking until they begin their formal school education.
 b. Children may see math as a set of rules and procedures, not as practical problem solving.
 c. Children will automatically apply their formal math learning to useful solutions in real life.
 d. Children are less likely to see connections between math and life using concrete objects.

42. What is the most effective way to facilitate children's comprehension of mathematics?
 a. To preserve mathematics as a discipline separate from other academic subjects and everyday life
 b. To allow children to find their own activities applying math rather than providing activities for them
 c. To help them connect and apply common math rules to many different life activities and processes
 d. To ask/answer questions and explain during formal math lessons, not confusing math with real life

43. Which of the following is true regarding children's development of the concept of symbolic representation?
 a. When young children engage in make-believe and pretend play, this is symbolic representation.
 b. Children do not develop this ability until they are old enough to engage in fully abstract thinking.
 c. Children first show this concept by reading, writing, and connecting written with spoken language.
 d. When young children first begin counting on their fingers, they have not yet developed this concept.

44. Suppose that a child in a preschool learning center enjoys sorting different rocks by color. Which of the following teacher practices is the best example of emphasis on connecting the informal math activity with formal math vocabulary?
 a. Telling the child s/he is classifying the rocks
 b. Asking the child how s/he is sorting the rocks
 c. Asking after s/he finishes other ways to sort
 d. These all exemplify the vocabulary emphasis

45. Which of these is true about having an awareness of patterns and relationships in the real world?
 a. Our understanding the basic structure of things is uninformed by it.
 b. It helps us understand series of events, but not predict future ones.
 c. It is unrelated to our basic feeling of confidence in the environment.
 d. It increases our self-efficacy about interacting with our environment.

46. Understanding patterns and relationships that exist in the environment helps children to understand which areas of mathematics?
    a. Geometrical forms
    b. Ordinal numbers
    c. Neither
    d. Both

47. Providing activities involving patterns and relationships helps prepare young children for academic math. Which of the following such activities is more likely to help them *create* patterns?
    a. Finding patterns in prints on fabric, paper, etc.
    b. Describing patterns in their own movements
    c. Stringing beads into necklaces, bracelets, etc.
    d. All these are equally good to create patterns

48. Which of the following is most accurate regarding young children's development of numeracy skills?
    a. Young children typically learn all of the number names before they learn to count.
    b. Young children typically learn to name all of the numbers and count simultaneously.
    c. Young children typically learn to count before they have learned all number names.
    d. Young children typically learn these two numeracy skills in individually varying order.

49. What is a correct statement about the development of number sense in young children?
    a. Children with developed number sense can count forward, but cannot necessarily count backward.
    b. Counting ability, number familiarity, and a good number sense enable children to add and subtract.
    c. Children who have developed number sense can break numbers down, but not reassemble them.
    d. Being able to identify relationships between/among numbers is an ability outside of number sense.

50. Which division of mathematics is most closely related to the development of spatial sense?
    a. Algebra
    b. Geometry
    c. Arithmetic
    d. All of these

51. Which of the following would be most effective to help young children learn geometry?
    a. Giving them hands-on activities manipulating concrete objects
    b. Giving the earliest geometric theorems for them to memorize
    c. Giving them everyday life activities only after they learn basics
    d. Giving them instructions for drawing geometric shape diagrams

52. Of the following, what statement is correct regarding practice in measurement for young children?
    a. Measurement is exclusively a formal method for quantifying sizes, time durations, weights, etc.
    b. Measurement is for both formal quantification and recognizing and finding real-life relationships.
    c. Measurement can only be accomplished by young children with standard measurement devices.
    d. Measurement practice for young children is unlikely to help them in learning about comparisons.

53. Which of these is correct regarding young children and the measurement of time?
    a. Young children typically develop an understanding of the abstract concept of time very early.
    b. Adults should not refer to periods of time with young children before they understand them.
    c. Using activities involving counting allows children to generalize these to the counting of time.
    d. Adults can say "yesterday, today, tomorrow" with young children and they will understand it.

54. Regarding young children's early comprehension of fractions, which of these is accurate?
    a. Children must know how many parts a unit is divided into, but not what comprises the unit.
    b. Children must know what makes a whole unit, but not into how many pieces it was divided.
    c. Children must know how many pieces a unit is divided into, but not if they are of equal size.
    d. Children must know what a whole unit is, how many parts there are, and if part sizes match.

55. Of the following, which is prerequisite for young children to understand before they can engage in accurately estimating basic measurements of quantities?
    a. Knowledge of math vocabulary words indicating estimation
    b. Knowledge of how to make predictions that are appropriate
    c. Knowledge of how to achieve estimates that are reasonable
    d. Knowledge of what relative quantities and comparisons are

56. Which of these is/are most representative of using statistics in everyday life to predict probabilities?
    a. An actuarial table in an insurance company
    b. A weather forecast for the chances of rain
    c. A chart comparing results of interventions
    d. Answers (A) and (B) represent probability

57. A teacher asks ten preschoolers to choose their favorite among four colors of foil stars. Five children pick gold; three choose silver; two select blue; and one picks red. The teacher then helps the student to stick the stars onto a paper chart with a separate row for each color:

GOLD ★ ★ ★ ★ ★
SILVER ★ ★ ★
BLUE ★ ★
RED ★

This activity supports which of the following early mathematics skills?
    a. Determining various properties of figures
    b. Applying mathematical formulas to shapes
    c. Collecting, organizing, and displaying data
    d. Intuitively identifying probability concepts

58. A teacher presents this figure and asks the class how many different rectangles they can find in it.
Which student response is correct?
    a. Andrea's answer, "Only one."
    b. Billy's answer, "There are four."
    c. Charlie's answer, "I found ten."
    d. Darlene's answer, "I count five."

59. Which of the following statements is an example of using ordinal numbers?
    a. "I am four years old and my brother Timmy is two years old."
    b. "I sit at the first table for lunch and my sister sits at the third."
    c. "I play on the junior soccer team. My shirt says number six."
    d. "Two-thirds of my math class are boys and one-third is girls."

60. A group of five- and six-year-olds watch a teacher demonstrate measuring things with a standard ruler. Some students want to know why the teacher aligns the number 0 on the ruler with the first edge of an object, instead of starting with the number 1 as they do when they count. Which choice is the best answer for the teacher to give?
    a. To tell them this is how the teacher learned to do it in school
    b. To tell them this is how we include the first inch on the ruler
    c. To tell them this is how we can use the most space on rulers
    d. To tell them this is how we follow standard ruler convention

61. Which level of shape perception do young children typically develop first?
    a. Recognizing shapes
    b. Naming the shapes
    c. Analysis of shapes
    d. All develop at once

62. A teacher regularly integrates math into everyday EC activities. By asking young children to help at snack time by putting one snack on each plate, which math skill is the teacher primarily engaging?
    a. 1:1 correspondence
    b. Practice in counting
    c. Shapes recognition
    d. Comparison of size

63. How can an EC teacher best facilitate children's development of math communication and literacy?
    a. By asking the children questions
    b. By observing children's behaviors
    c. By lecturing to model language use
    d. By having children write about math

64. Preschoolers' development of spatial awareness will later support their comprehension of which areas of math the most?
    a. Arithmetic and algebra
    b. Geometry and physics
    c. Arithmetic and physics
    d. Geometry and algebra

65. Of the following, which preschool activity is most related to learning 1:1 correspondence?
    a. Being able to name all printed numbers on sight
    b. The ability to count numbers both up and down
    c. Counting out pennies to match a written number
    d. These all relate the same to 1:1 correspondence

66. Which of the following is a rational number?
    a. The value of pi (π)
    b. Square root of 2 (√2)
    c. Any decimal number
    d. 9,731,245/42,754,021

Social Studies

67. Which of the following levels of self-awareness do children tend to develop earliest?
    a. Situation
    b. Permanence
    c. Identification
    d. Differentiation

68. Of the following, which can babies typically do from birth?
    a. Recognize photos and mirror images as themselves
    b. Systematically imitate facial expressions of others
    c. Distinguish between internal and external stimuli
    d. Systematically reach for and touch seen objects

69. In EC development in the area of interpersonal interactions, which do children typically develop first?
    a. Autonomy/independence
    b. Trusting/mistrusting others
    c. A sense of initiative or guilt
    d. Make-believe/pretending

70. What is true about instructing children in conflict resolution skills and processes?
    a. Conflict resolution can be taught to children who are as young as eighteen months.
    b. Children can only understand these concepts at school ages (six years and up).
    c. Conflict resolution instruction has never been attempted with young children.
    d. Children taught conflict mediation/resolution are unlikely to generalize these.

71. Of these four parenting styles described by psychologists, which is considered the ideal?
    a. Authoritative
    b. Authoritarian
    c. Permissive
    d. Uninvolved

72. According to family systems theory, when one member of a family is consistently identified as the family peacemaker and another is viewed as the family clown, these most reflect which system component?
    a. Boundaries
    b. Roles
    c. Rules
    d. Equilibrium

73. A child whose family comes from a collectivist culture is most likely to value:
    a. Competition.
    b. Independence.
    c. Cooperation.
    d. Uniqueness.

74. A family moves to America from another country with a very different culture. They discard their native cultural practices and adopt American customs. This is an example of:
    a. Accommodation
    b. Adaptation
    c. Acculturation
    d. Assimilation

75. Which of the following is most accurate about cultural competence in educational professionals?
    a. Hiring language interpreters and translators will assure cultural competence.
    b. Hiring educational staff with racial diversity will ensure cultural competence.
    c. Hiring highly culturally self-aware educators will create cultural competence.
    d. Hiring these plus educator communication skills creates cultural competence.

76. Research comparing American Latino and White parent beliefs has found that:
    a. Most White parents believe that children's learning capacities are set at birth.
    b. Most White and Latino parents share the same beliefs about learning capacity.
    c. Most Latino parents believe children's learning capacities are fixed from birth.
    d. Most Latino parents highly value early intervention and stimulation of learning.

77. Which statement is most accurate regarding variations among culturally diverse U.S. parents in whether or how often they read to their young children?
    a. Parents who succeeded despite not being read to as children value reading to children even more.
    b. Some cultures with oral traditions tell stories and sing to their children more than reading to them.
    c. Educators can easily influence parents whose culture does not value/prioritize reading to children.
    d. Parents not seeing school readiness and success as benefits can still be taught to read to children.

78. Which statement is true of findings about culturally diverse parental views of child development milestones in America?
    a. Parents in America from different cultures expect their children to reach milestones at different ages.
    b. Anglo, Filipino, and Puerto Rican parents in America differ in age expectations only for sleeping lone.
    c. Anglo, Filipino, and Puerto Rican parents in America expect children to eat solid food at the same age.
    d. The only age expectation shared by all parents is when their children should sleep through the night.

79. Land is typically more expensive in urban areas than in rural areas. Which geography concept does this reflect?
    a. Location
    b. Distance
    c. Pattern
    d. Interaction

80. As used in geographical maps, which of the following is a synonym for the term *latitude?*
    a. Longitude
    b. Parallel
    c. Meridian
    d. Coordinate

81. Which of the following is correct regarding common types of graphs?
    a. A pie chart shows differences in quantities over time.
    b. A bar graph can compare quantities but not over time.
    c. A line graph clarifies how amounts change over time.
    d. A number column makes patterns and trends clearer.

82. Of these materials, which can teachers use to help students develop chronological thinking?
    a. Only history books can be used for this.
    b. Biographies can also serve this function.
    c. Historical literature can be used for this.
    d. These are all good chronology materials.

83. To teach citizenship at the EC level, what purposes of laws and rules should teachers help young children to understand?
    a. People who are employed in positions of authority wield unlimited powers.
    b. Individual citizens determine their own responsibilities separately from laws.
    c. Individuals and groups make up our government to create and enforce laws.
    d. Life and society are unpredictable, insecure and disorderly, despite any laws.

Science

84. Young children develop many basic science concepts through everyday activities. Of the following, which activity is most related to the development of measurement concepts?
    a. Fitting wooden pegs into holes with matching shapes in a toy
    b. Pouring sand from one container into a differently sized one
    c. Seeing how many coins they have accrued in their piggy bank
    d. Separating toys into piles of cars, trucks, animals, people, etc.

85. Which is the best definition of an informal learning experience for learning basic science concepts?
    a. A child chooses what to do, and an adult provides some intervention
    b. A child chooses what to do spontaneously without adult intervention
    c. A child engages in an activity which is chosen and directed by an adult
    d. A child engages in a group activity assigned by the preschool teacher

86. Of the following actions, which best represents the science process skill of Inference?
    a. Formulating new hypotheses based on experimental results
    b. Finding patterns and meaning in the results of experiments
    c. Identifying properties of things/situations using the senses
    d. Reporting experimental results and conclusions to others

87. Which of the following gases is known as a compound gas?
    a. Oxygen
    b. Nitrogen
    c. Ammonia
    d. Hydrogen

88. When we look at a straw in a glass of water, the straw appears broken or bent at the waterline. This appearance is a function of:
    a. Scattering.
    b. Absorption.
    c. Reflection.
    d. Refraction.

89. When materials that are attracted by magnets align at right angles to the lines of the magnetic force field, the name for this is:
    a. Magnetic induction
    b. Ferromagnetism
    c. Paramagnetism
    d. Diamagnetism

90. Which statement is correct regarding the phenomenon of magnetism?
    a. Opposite poles of magnets repel each other.
    b. The like poles of magnets attract each other.
    c. Magnets can attract/repel without touching.
    d. Magnets work beyond their magnetic fields.

91. For electricity to flow and move, it requires which of these?
    a. A generator and an insulator
    b. A generator and a conductor
    c. A conductor and an insulator
    d. Electricity needs all of these

92. Heat is transmitted through solid materials via:
    a. Conduction.
    b. Convection.
    c. Radiation.
    d. All three.

93. Newton's First Law of Motion states that:
    a. An object at rest tends to stay at rest unless an opposing force changes this.
    b. An object stays at rest or in motion unless/until an opposing force changes it.
    c. An object in motion tends to stay in motion until an opposing force changes it.
    d. For every action that take place, there is an equal and opposite reaction to it.

94. In our environment, the most common medium that conducts sound waves is:
    a. Solid.
    b. Liquid.
    c. Gaseous.
    d. All these.

95. Which type of rock typically forms on the surface of the earth in cumulative layers?
    a. Igneous
    b. Obsidian
    c. Metamorphic
    d. Sedimentary

96. Which organisms depend *most* on light to survive?
    a. Undersea plants
    b. Mammalians
    c. Land plants
    d. Humans

97. Which of the following have a simple life cycle, without a metamorphosis?
    a. Frogs
    b. Newts
    c. Grasshoppers
    d. Human beings

98. Of the following insects, which undergo a complete metamorphosis during their life cycle?
    a. Mosquitos
    b. Butterflies
    c. Dragonflies
    d. Grasshoppers

99. The way that plants reproduce is:
    a. Asexual.
    b. Sexual.
    c. Both.
    d. Neither.

100. In an ecosystem, its abiotic factors:
    a. Are alive.
    b. Are not alive.
    c. Do not affect living organisms.
    d. Include some microorganisms.

Health and Physical Education

101. The American Recovery and Reinvestment Act (2009) includes funding or the U.S. Dept. of Health and Human Services to prevent chronic disease. This initiative targets which of the following as the most preventable causes of disability and death?
    a. Obesity and tobacco use
    b. Alcohol and tobacco use
    c. Alcohol and drug abuse
    d. Obesity and diabetes

102. Which statement is true about children and environmental health risks?
    a. Children's body systems are more robust and resilient than adults' are.
    b. Children are liable to be more vulnerable to environmental health risks.
    c. Children take in fewer toxins from the air, water, and food than adults.
    d. Children's normal behaviors expose them to fewer toxins than adults'.

103. A part of which of these human body systems regulates the body temperature?
    a. Lymphatic
    b. Circulatory
    c. Integumentary
    d. Musculoskeletal

104. Which of these causes our hearts to beat?
    a. The autonomic nervous system
    b. The parasympathetic system
    c. The sympathetic system
    d. Both A and C but not B

105. Which lobe of the human brain is associated with processing visual information?
    a. The frontal lobe
    b. The parietal lobe
    c. The occipital lobe
    d. The temporal lobe

106. Which human gland performs both endocrine and exocrine functions?
    a. The thyroid
    b. The salivary
    c. The pituitary
    d. The pancreas

107. Prenatal, infant, and child motor development progresses from the head down. This is known as:
   a. Cephalocaudal development
   b. Proximodistal development
   c. Mediolateral development
   d. Intellectual development

108. Which of the following is true about young children's physical activity?
   a. Children's motor skills generally develop later than their language skills.
   b. Attempting and succeeding at physical challenges enhances self-efficacy.
   c. Physical activity develops children's physical rather than cognitive skills.
   d. Only language and arts skills can give children means of self-expression.

109. Which of these is true about the National Association for Sport and Physical Education (NASPE)'s national standards for physical education?
   a. They include learning and executing physical activities rather than concepts.
   b. They include conducting physical activities rather than showing motor skills.
   c. They include understanding concepts as well as engaging in physical activity.
   d. They include valuing physical and personal but not social benefits of activity.

110. The World Health Organization (WHO) recommends at least _____ of moderate to vigorous physical activity for children aged five to seventeen.
   a. 15 minutes a day
   b. 30 minutes a day
   c. 1 hour every day
   d. 1 hour per week

The Arts

111. Of the following, which is correct regarding arts education in early childhood?
   a. EC teachers should focus on assigning separate art activities so children realize art's importance.
   b. EC teachers enhance learning and comprehension by integrating art into the overall curriculum.
   c. EC teachers are told by many state standards to integrate art into units but not whole curricula.
   d. EC teachers who assign art process activities should be giving children any rules or steps in advance.

112. An EC teacher gives children an art activity of illustrating and labeling plants or animals by name that they learned about in a science unit. This best exemplifies which learning application of art?
   a. Using art to build their language skills and vocabularies
   b. Developing skills of color recognition and discrimination
   c. Developing awareness of line, shape, color, and texture
   d. Using art to express feelings and thoughts, and tell stories

113. When planning an art project or activity for young children, which should the teacher do first?
   a. Construct a simple prototype of the intended product.
   b. Establish which particular concept s/he wants to teach.
   c. Determine learning objectives for the children to meet.
   d. Identify teacher objectives for planning and instruction.

114. Which of these statements is true about the context of a given work of art?
 a. An artwork's context and its function are separate, unrelated aspects.
 b. The context of a given work of art is primarily determined by the artist.
 c. An artwork's function relies on context which is half artist, half viewer.
 d. The context of a given work of art is primarily determined by a viewer.

115. In the artistic process of creating art, which step comes first?
 a. Making, evaluating, and refining the product
 b. Planning: researching, experimenting, design
 c. Presenting by exhibiting or performing the art
 d. Imagining ideas and feelings to express in art

116. While students are engaged in creating their own artworks, their teacher shows them other students' work. The teacher's doing this facilitates:
 a. Generalization/transfer from the creation process to the response process.
 b. Generalization/transfer from the response process to the creation process.
 c. Generalization/transfer from an analysis process to an interpreting process.
 d. Generalization/transfer from the interpretation into the evaluation process.

117. Which of the following is defined as a primary color?
 a. Orange
 b. Yellow
 c. Green
 d. Purple

118. The sound wave frequency of a musical note is its:
 a. Tempo
 b. Melody
 c. Pitch
 d. Rhythm

119. The waltz is traditionally associated most with which time signature?
 a. 2/2
 b. 2/4
 c. 4/4
 d. 3/4

120. Among art's organizing principles, Beethoven's *Symphony No. 5* makes striking use of which principle related specifically to its main theme?
 a. Movement
 b. Repetition
 c. Contrast
 d. Pattern

16. B: The 3N strategy does use scaffolding, i.e., temporary support that the teacher provides to help young students achieve tasks at levels higher than their current literacy status. Scaffolding is gradually withdrawn as students become more proficient until they can achieve these tasks independently. 3N *does* incorporate informal assessment of literacy levels (A): the first, "Notice" step involves the teacher's noticing each individual student's current level of literacy skills. It *does* integrate reflection (C): the third, "Narrate" step involves the teacher's reflecting on what the student does. This strategy *is* adaptable to young children's games (D): various literacy games designed for young children apply the 3N strategy.

17. C: The most helpful strategy for discerning which of two homonyms (sound-alike words) is correct without knowing the spelling is its surrounding context of the sentence, paragraph, and/or book and subject matter. For example, "Mexico cedes land" and "Mexico seeds land" sound the same, but if the context continues "to the United States," the meaning of "cedes" applies. Pictures (A) help children identify unknown words rather than differentiate homonyms. Phonics (B) help students sound out unfamiliar words, not differentiate meanings. Grammar (D) can help when one homonym is a verb and the other a noun, for example; but "cedes" and "seeds" are the same part of speech with different meanings, so grammar alone does not help as much as context.

18. D: Good children's books should feature plots that are well-constructed, and are original but not incredible. Narrative books should feature story characters who are believable, which includes their changing (A) and growing as a result of their experiences like real people do, rather than staying the same throughout the story. Adults choosing children's literature should seek books with themes of value to children, but avoid books with overtly moralistic themes (B). Likewise they should avoid books that promote racial, gender, and other stereotypes (C).

19. C: These features are most characteristic of traditional literature, which has been adapted by authors from oral traditions including folklore, epics, fables, proverbs, and fairy tales. The modern fantasy (A) genre, which includes modern-day fairy tales and tells imaginative tales, may use traditional literature themes as its foundation, but is original writing by authors such as Hans Christian Andersen, Lewis Carroll, and E.B. White. Picture books (B) combine text and pictures, which help beginning students learn to read by supplementing words with illustrations. Poetry books (D) contain poems rather than prose writing.

20. B: If a young child cannot break down a word into its component phonemes, this represents a deficit in phonological and/or phonemic awareness, which will cause reading difficulties. Likewise, the inability to do the reverse and blend individual phonemes to form words (C) is a sign the child will have trouble reading. Young children with good phonological and phonemic awareness can both identify *and* form rhymes (A). To learn to read well, they should also be able to count the syllables in a word and use phonetic spellings (by sound) for new/unfamiliar words (D).

21. A: Conversational English is much *less* difficult (A) for ESL students to learn because it is much less demanding of them cognitively. Most often, academic underachievement in ESL students is caused by deficits in academic, not conversational English (B). The disparity in ease of developing these separate skill sets—basic, everyday-life interpersonal communication skills in conversational English vs. the complex-compound syntax and vocabularies specific to math, science, social studies, and other content areas in academic English—is apparent in the fact that while most ESL children develop conversational English within about two years of living in English-speaking settings, they take at least five to seven years to develop academic English (D).

22. D: A word wall uses visual illustrations of vocabulary words and the concepts they represent, and includes additional words, concepts, and pictures related to the main words and pictures to enrich vocabulary and relational thinking. The teacher would be most responsible for creating the word wall, using it in lessons/activities, and instructing/assisting young children in its use. The children themselves can and will repeatedly sing the same familiar song (A) and repeat the same rhymes and chants (B), which enhance vocabulary development for both native English-speaking and ESL students. Stories (C) may be read live by teachers, or readings may be recorded. Either way, the children play the same role of listening to repeated readings.

23. C: While *some* children's reading lacks fluency due to deficits in their word-decoding abilities, this is not *always* (A) the case: some children simply need more reading practice to develop fluency. Children's motivation to read (B) *is* affected by their reading fluency: when reading is laborious, children do not enjoy it and avoid reading; when reading is easy, children enjoy it and want to read. Fluency has much *greater* impact (D) on the performance of students in higher grades, when the volume of reading required of them in school is exponentially greater.

24. B: If a child can repeat the factual elements of how a story ended, but cannot explain why this ending occurred, this may show that the child cannot reason about cause and effect, logic, and sequencing in the material s/he has read; and/or lacks the expressive language skills to explain. Wondering about characters' reasons for their actions (A) indicates comprehension, not its lack: readers with good comprehension will speculate about character motivations, and will also try to predict future events in a book (C) before reading of them. Relating reading matter to one's own life (D) and pre-existing knowledge also does not indicate comprehension problems, but rather good reading comprehension.

25. A: Students with dyslexia tend to perform much worse than their intelligence and knowledge would indicate on objective formats like multiple-choice tests. They are likely to have *equal* amounts of difficulty with reading short function words (e.g., *an, on, in*) as with reading long, multisyllabic words (B). While they do have trouble with fluid thinking, e.g., thinking "on the spot" to produce spoken and/or written verbal responses, they also have equal difficulty with retaining and/or retrieving names, dates, random lists, phone numbers, and other information through rote memorization and recall (C). Students with dyslexia typically have more trouble understanding words in isolation than in context (D), because they rely on the surrounding context to comprehend word meanings.

26. B: Once children have learned the basic rules and principles for spelling in their native language, they can usually figure out how to spell words that are new to them when they hear them spoken. As children accrue experience in communicating with language, they notice basic patterns in letter combinations, syllables, common word roots, prefixes, suffixes, endings, etc., so much of their knowledge of spelling patterns comes through incidental learning (A). Also, children usually can read words that they can spell (C). Therefore, not only do their reading and writing skills support correct spelling, but reciprocally, good spelling skills also support children's reading and writing (D).

27. C: Linguists have found through research studies that not only do preschool children invent spellings for words before they have learned their actual spellings, but moreover, preschoolers from diverse backgrounds all choose the same phonetic spellings, at a rate higher than can be attributed to chance (D) or adult influences (B). The researchers have concluded that through these common invented, phonetic spellings, young children demonstrate comprehension—not a lack thereof (A)—of the phonetic characteristics of words, and of how conventional word spellings symbolize these characteristics.

28. D: Five stages identified in children's writing development are: Scribbling and drawing (A), wherein they hold crayons/pencils in their fists and explore line, space, and form; Letter-like forms and shapes (D), wherein they understand that written forms symbolize meanings and begin drawing circles, squares, and other shapes, drawing figures and asking parents what they "say." In the Letters (B) stage, children can form letter shapes, usually starting with consonants, and enjoy writing their own name initials. They only gradually develop understanding of the sounds represented by the letters. In the Letters and spaces (C) stage, children develop word concepts and space correctly between words. The fifth stage is Conventional writing and spelling, including correct punctuation and purposeful writing.

29. D: Research into literacy development reveals that improvement in students' writing skills improves their overall learning ability, just as improvement in their reading skills also does. Expressing ideas, thoughts, and feelings (A) is *one* purpose of student writing, but not the only or main one. Another purpose is persuasion of the reader audience to agree with the writer's point of view and/or believe the writer's assertions—again, not the only or main purpose (B), but one of various purposes. Research also finds not only that improving student reading skills improves their writing, but *also* that, reciprocally, improving student writing skills improves their reading (C).

30. C: POWER stands for Planning, Organization, Writing, Editing, and Rewriting. The first, Planning, step is particularly important because many students tend simply to plunge into writing without making any plans in advance for choosing a good topic, researching and/or reading on the topic, considering which information will appeal to the reader audience, and writing down all their ideas on the topic.

31. B: The category of Message Quality includes understanding the concepts of signs and symbols, of communicating a message; copying messages; repeating formulaic sentence patterns (e.g., "This is a...."); attempting to use writing to record one's own ideas; and successfully composing writing. Writing two related sentences with punctuation (A) and writing a story with paragraphs and two themes (C) are progressive levels of development falling into the Language Level category. Spacing correctly between written words (D) is a level of the Directional Principles category.

32. A: First, a child typically shows no knowledge of the correct direction in which to write (left-right, top-bottom in English); then partial knowledge, e.g., *either* left-right *or* top-bottom *or* moving from the upper right at the end of one line to the left for the next line; then reversed writing direction; then correct directionality; then correct direction plus correct spacing between words.

33. B: How appropriate the content of a student's composition is reflects function rather than form. Composition length (A), word usage (C), and spelling (D) in a student's composition are all reflections of the composition's form rather than its function.

34. C: This sentence contains the grammatical error of a misplaced modifier. The modifying phrase "a great animal lover" does NOT modify "his pets" but him (e.g., "A great animal lover, *he had* pets including...."). Choice (A) contains a spelling error: "friend" is misspelled. A common student error is to transpose vowel combinations like this. Choice (B) has a punctuation error: these two independent clauses should be separated by a semicolon, not a comma. (In this example, a colon would also be acceptable, but not a comma, which creates a run-on sentence.) Choice (D) has a capitalization error: "South" and "West" are only capitalized when used as names, e.g., "the wild West" or "the sunny South," but when used as directions are lowercase.

35. D: Educational experts find that children, like adults, are more motivated to participate in activities that are exciting to them than to engage in activities they find uninteresting or boring. They also advise that to sustain children's enthusiasm for writing, teachers should provide diverse writing activities rather than getting stuck in a predictable routine (C) of always using the same ones (A). They note that children's familiarity with the subject they write about increases their motivation rather than decreasing it (B).

36. D: Studies find these areas of conditions contributing to writing motivation: promoting student beliefs about writing's functionality (A); giving students authentic (true-to-life) writing activities that will engage them in writing (B); establishing a positive emotional environment wherein students can write (C); and creating a context for students that supports writing. Researchers also find the teacher's perceptions of writing to be equally critical for achieving all of these conditions to motivate student writing.

Mathematics

37. C: Students apply logical reasoning to solve both usual, everyday problems and unusual, novel problems they encounter. Developing problem-solving skills not only helps students to think mathematically; it also develops their social skills (A) and language skills (B) when they collaborate to solve problems in math questions, in other school subjects, and in real life; and when they communicate, compare, and discuss their solutions. Children are naturally curious about how everyday problems can be solved: rather than having to teach them this interest (D), teachers can take advantage of this naturally existing motivation by asking them to propose problems; to propose solutions to problems and explain how they reached them; and asking questions about problems and solutions.

38. B: Emotional and behavioral self-regulation skills are important components of problem-solving abilities in students. Without these, students would not have the patience, persistence, and flexibility to keep trying alternative solutions if their first solution fails (D). Another characteristic of problem-solving behavior is to formulate hypotheses first and then test them for accuracy, not vice versa (A). An additional characteristic of good problem-solvers is to be willing to take reasonable risks (C).

39. A: Whether they actually introduce physical objects for the youngest children, or simply describe concrete objects in oral story problems, adults should always ask young children these in terms of concrete objects. For example, asking, "two + two = what?" may be too abstract; but asking, "If you have two grapes and I give you two more, how many will you have?" facilitates children's ability to manipulate numbers via seeing them as familiar items. Adults can start with favorite foods and then add problems using toys, cars, grocery items, etc. According to experts, adults should not restrict such games to grade levels (B): young children can address any scenario for which they can form mental images. Adults are also advised to include occasional harder problems, e.g., involving division remainders, bigger numbers, negative number results, etc., rather than making 100 percent of them simple (C). They should also ask young children guiding questions (the Socratic method) to help them solve problems themselves, rather than just telling them an answer (D).

40. D: Experts recommend asking children "why?" questions; *not* expecting certain answers (A) but being open to whatever ideas they may produce; *not* asking questions without permitting or attending to children's answers (B); allowing children enough time to think about what their answers might be rather than demanding immediate responses (C); and listening attentively to the original, sometimes unique, answers that the children come up with on their own by thinking through the questions. This supports children in developing their reasoning skills, which are vital to problem solving, math, and science.

41. B: One common event when children begin school is that, through formal math lessons, they view academic math as a group of rules and steps to follow rather than a body of knowledge they can apply to solve real-life problems. Children *do* mathematical thinking before school (A); it is just intuitive rather than formal mathematical thought. As evidenced by the accuracy of (B), children will *not* automatically apply their formal math learning to useful solutions in real life (C); however, teachers can help them learn to do this. One way they can facilitate this transition and application is to provide children with familiar concrete objects that they can manipulate during math lessons, which makes them *more,* not less (D) likely to see connections between math and real life.

42. C: Parents and other adults can best help children understand math concepts and procedures by helping them realize how these are applied in many different activities, including other academic subjects like the sciences, arts, and music and a variety of everyday life activities. They should NOT isolate math from life and other school subjects (A). They should NOT just let children do whatever they please and hope that they apply math in these activities (B); instead, they can engage them in activities applying math concepts, like sorting when putting away groceries or setting the table. They should not restrict working on math comprehension to formal math lessons (D), but seek and find math concepts and practices in everyday life routines and events. This will help them understand math better, as well as apply it in practical ways.

43. A: One of the earliest evidences of children's developing the idea of symbolic representation—i.e., the concept that things like numbers, letters, words, and objects can be used to represent other things—is their engaging in make-believe and pretend play (e.g., a toy horse represents a real horse; a block is used to represent a cell phone; a stick becomes a laser sword, etc.). Children develop this ability long before they develop fully abstract thought (B). Make-believe and pretend play develop *sooner than* reading, writing, and the alphabetic principle (C), which also employs the concept of symbolic representation. Another example that young children *have* developed symbolic representation is their counting on their fingers (D).

44. A: When the teacher supplies the student with the formal math vocabulary word "classifying", s/he is emphasizing the connection of the child's informal math activity of sorting rocks with the formal math vocabulary word that describes it. Asking the child how s/he is sorting the rocks (B) is a better example of the teacher's emphasizing math communication than vocabulary (by having the child explain). Asking, after the child finishes sorting rocks, what other ways s/he could sort them (C) is a better example of emphasizing problem-solving skills than math vocabulary. Therefore (D) is incorrect.

45. D: Being aware that patterns (regular repetitions) and relationships (associations between/among things) exist in the world affords us greater self-efficacy about our interacting with the environment, as well as increasing our sense of confidence in the environment itself (C). This awareness not only helps us to understand sequences of events; it moreover enables us to predict the next event in the series before it occurs (B). Having an awareness of patterns and relationships in things also informs our understanding of the basic structure of those things (A).

46. D: Children will be able to understand both geometrical forms (A), i.e., lines, shapes, arcs, and curves, and ordinal numbers (B) we use in counting if they first understand the patterns and relationships existing around them in everyday life. Therefore, (C) is incorrect. Patterns consist of regular repetitions or recurrences in things, and relationships consist of associations or connections between/among things. We tend to see these where they exist, impose them where they do not (like seeing pictures in natural cloud formations, wood grains, etc.), and create products featuring them.

47. C: Stringing beads (or hollow pasta) into necklaces and bracelets allows children to alternate different colors to create simple patterns. As they grow, adults can help them create more complex patterns, using more colors and varying how many they use of each color. Finding patterns in prints (A) and describing their and other children's movement patterns (B) when they dance to music, hop, skip, jump, run, beat drums, pluck strings or press keys on simple musical instruments, etc., are more likely to help children *identify* patterns, which is important per se and as preparation for creating patterns. Therefore (D) is incorrect.

48. C: Normally developing young children typically learn to count before they have learned the names of all of the numbers. They do NOT typically learn all number names before learning to count (A). They do NOT typically acquire both skills at the same time (B). And they do NOT typically vary individually in the order (D) of acquiring these skills.

49. B: When young children have learned how to count, have become familiar with numbers, and have developed good number sense, these three achievements will enable them to add and subtract numbers—i.e., to do beginning arithmetic computations. Children with developed number sense are able to count both forward *and* backward (A). They can also break numbers down into their components, *and* reassemble them (C). Being able to identify relationships between or among numbers *is* an ability that is included in number sense (D).

50. B: Geometry is the division of mathematics that studies spatial forms like shapes, lines, arcs, and curves, and their properties and motions. As such, it is most closely related to the development of spatial sense. Algebra (A) studies mathematical sets, operations, and relations using numbers, letters (e.g., *x, y, n,* etc.), and symbols. Arithmetic (C) is the basic numerical computations we use with numbers, e.g., addition, subtraction, multiplication, division, etc. Neither of these focuses on spatial forms as geometry does. Therefore, all of these (D) is an incorrect choice.

51. A: Young children need concrete objects to manipulate to learn geometry concepts. In early childhood, they think concretely and thus need to see, touch, and manipulate real things to help them understand abstract concepts. Therefore, their memorizing theorems (B) at this age, when most children cannot even read let alone understand them, would be ineffective. Children should be given everyday life activities that teach geometric concepts—e.g., cutting their sandwiches into different geometric shapes, naming these for them, and letting them assemble and/or rearrange the pieces—*before* rather than after (C) they learn formal geometry basics, as activities that are part of daily life are relevant to young children and an effective way to teach concepts. Instructions to draw geometric diagrams (D) are more appropriate when children are older and have learned geometry concepts from interacting with solid objects, and also have better-developed fine motor skills. Certainly adults can help them draw shapes, but this should not be a first and/or isolated exercise.

52. B: Measurement is not only a formal system for quantifying amounts and numbers that specify sizes, times, weights, etc. (A). It is also used informally in everyday life. As such, it is a valuable skill that young children can use to recognize and find relationships among real-world objects, outside of academic exercises. Young children are not restricted to standardized rulers, scales, clocks, calendars, etc. (C). They also practice measuring things using whatever is available, e.g., comparing objects to the length of their fingers, hands, feet, etc., or to pieces of string; comparing the heft of an object to that of a block or other toy for weight; comparing how long someone is gone to the duration of a TV show, etc. Measuring practice *does* help children learn to compare object sizes/weights and time periods (D).

53. C: Adults can help young children understand the concepts that time passes and is counted and measured by engaging them in counting activities, getting them used to counting in general, telling them how much time various activities took, and showing them the second hand on a clock or watch and counting "One second, two seconds, three...." Young children typically have NOT yet developed understanding of the abstract concept of time (A). However, adults *should* refer to time periods with young children, even before they understand these (B). For example, they can tell children, "You may play for five more minutes before bedtime." Making such references will aid young children's eventual realization of the passage of time. But young children will typically *not* understand such abstract concepts as yesterday/today/tomorrow (D); adults can use more concrete referents, e.g., "after supper" or "before bedtime" until children are older.

54. D: To understand fractions, children must know all of these things: what makes up a particular whole unit; how many pieces that unit is divided into; and whether the pieces are all of the same size or not. Knowing the number of parts but not what makes up the unit (A); knowing what comprises the whole unit, but not how many pieces into which it has been divided (B); or knowing both what makes up the whole unit and how many pieces it has been divided into, but not knowing whether the pieces are equal in size or not (C) will not allow children to comprehend the concept of fractions. For example, a child will not understand the idea of thirds if something is divided into three parts of *unequal* size, because each piece is not equal to one-third of the whole.

55. D: To be able to make accurate estimates of quantities, children must first understand relative and comparative concepts such as bigger than, smaller than, more of, less of, etc. The process of estimating numbers and amounts in lieu of actual exact measurements helps young children to *learn* math vocabulary words (A) like *around, about, more than, less than,* etc., rather than vice versa. By practicing estimation, children also learn how to make predictions appropriately (B) and attain reasonable estimates (C), rather than the other way around.

56. D: Both an insurance company's actuarial table (A) and a weather forecast for the chances of rain (B) predict the probability or likelihood of something happening—for an individual's illness, injury, or death by a given age (A), or for precipitation to occur in a given day or week (B). A chart comparing the results of different interventions (C) organizes and allows people to interpret data related to which method was more or less effective with certain populations rather than predicting the likelihood of any occurrence.

57. C: By having each child select his/her favorite star color, the teacher is giving the children experience with collecting things the way adults collect data (i.e., pieces of information). By having them place all stars of each color in separate columns, the teacher gives the children experience with organizing the data they have collected. By labeling each column with one color and placing each star in the corresponding color column, the teacher is giving the children experience with displaying the data they have collected and organized. Determining figure properties (A) would be better illustrated by an activity involving differentiating triangles, octagons, circles, etc. Applying formulas to shapes (B) would work better with school-age children; for example, practice in multiplying length by width to find area. Intuitively identifying probability (D) might involve having the children predict how many of them will choose each star color with the example given.

58. C: Charlie's response of ten rectangles is correct. The entire figure is itself a rectangle, making one (A). The four squares within it (B) that Billy saw are also rectangles, making the five (D) that Darlene counted. In addition, connected squares create more rectangles: there are three two-square rectangles and two three-square rectangles. Three and two make five more, for a total of ten.

59. B: Ordinal numbers do not indicate the quantity of things but rather their order in a series or set, i.e., the rank or position of each member—the first and third tables here. Choice (A) is an example of cardinal numbers, which indicate quantity or how many—here, four years and two years old. Choice (C) is an example of a nominal number, i.e., one that indicates neither rank nor quantity, but rather a number used as a name to identify something—here, the shirt number of a team player (six). Choice (D) is an example of using rational numbers, i.e., divisions/ratios of integers, or more simply, fractions—two-thirds and one-third here.

60. B: The most accurate, and therefore the best answer in this case, is to tell the students that only starting the measurement with zero allows the first inch to be included/counted. Telling them this is how the teacher learned to do it (A) or that this is a convention of standard rulers to be followed (D) do not offer any explanation of the logic behind measurement; moreover, it is not accurate to say this is done merely to conform. It is equally inaccurate to tell young students this is a way to maximize the use of ruler space (C). Such answers fail to address the central concept that measuring quantities does not begin with a pre-existing quantity of 1.

61. A: Children develop shape perception in a chronological sequence, rather than all at once (D). At their youngest, children can identify simple shapes by sight. Only once their linguistic and cognitive skills develop further do they learn the words to name these shapes (B). When they reach the third level of shape perception, children no longer rely only on intuition and appearances, but can also analyze shapes (C), so that they can recognize even a triangle, for example, which is crooked, distorted, taller/thinner/wider than usual, by its constant properties (e.g., three sides, which may be of equal or different lengths).

62. A: The teacher is engaging the math skills of 1:1 correspondence by directing the children to place one object on each plate. Practice in counting (B) would be engaged more by, for example, asking children when they line up for an activity, "Who is first? Second? Third?" etc., or by asking them to "count off" in line ("One, two, three...."). Recognizing shapes (C) could be engaged by, for example, asking children when they play with blocks what shape each block has. Size comparison (D) could be engaged by asking children which block or other toy is bigger or smaller than another one.

63. A: EC teachers can learn much about how young children are learning new mathematical concepts through observing their behaviors (B); but to help them develop math communication, realize the linguistic functions of math, and develop overall literacy, teachers must also elicit spoken expressions from children about their own knowledge and thought processes. They can do this by asking children questions (e.g., "What shape is this? How about this one? How are these shapes different? Why/how do you think they are different?" etc.). They can then use children's responses to elicit additional expressions from them. While teachers can certainly model language use for children (C) in their speech, including conversations, discussions, directions, and lessons, lecturing (C) is not the best method, especially with young children. Assigning writing about math (D) supports children's reading and writing development and supports literacy too, but is not a substitute for questioning and eliciting further responses.

64. B: Spatial awareness is a foundation most related to later understanding the mathematical areas of geometry, which deals with shapes, lines, and other forms and their movements, and physics, which deals with the laws of objects in motion, at rest, etc. Arithmetic {(A), (C)} deals with basic numerical computations, and algebra {(A), (D)} deals with sets of numbers and their relationships, including letter symbols, equations, and formulas, as for solving unknown quantities, etc.

65. C: Young children's learning to name numbers (A) is comparable to their learning to name alphabet letters. This reflects the understanding that written/printed symbols represent numerical or alphabetic concepts. Learning to count (B) reflects an additional math skill. But neither of these is the same as understanding that symbols also represent concrete objects found in the real world, which constitutes a major cognitive progression. This understanding is demonstrated by young children when they can view a printed/written number and then count out the corresponding number of objects (like pennies). Therefore, (D) is not true.

66. D: 9,731,245/42,754,021 is a fraction. Any number that can be written as a ratio or fraction is rational. The value of pi (π) (A) is an irrational number, as is the square root of 2 ($\sqrt{2}$) (B), because their numbers to the right of the decimal point continue indefinitely without resolution. Therefore, any decimal number (C) is NOT rational; only decimal numbers that end, and thus can be written as fractions or ratios, are rational.

Social Studies

67. D: Newborns demonstrate body differentiation in their rooting and orienting responses for nursing, and young children learn to differentiate their mirror images from other people. Typically, situation (A) follows differentiation: children progress from differentiating self to realizing that their bodies/selves are physically situated in space, and that their mirror reflections are unique to their selves. Subsequently, children develop identification (C), e.g., knowing one's mirror image is "me" as demonstrated by their touching something applied to their face when they see it in a mirror. Thereafter, they develop permanence (B), the recognition that their self is permanent across space and time. (The fifth level of self-awareness is "meta"-self-awareness or self-consciousness, allowing perception of the self from others' perspectives.)

68. C: From birth, infants can tell the difference between their own bodies and the environment around them. They can differentiate between internal stimulation from touching themselves and external stimulation from others touching them. Children typically develop the recognition of photos and mirror images as symbolic representations of themselves (A) by the time they are around two years old. Babies typically develop systematic imitation of others' facial expressions (B), gestures, and other movements around the age of two months. They usually develop the ability of systematically reaching for and touching things they see (D), which requires eye-hand coordination, around the age of four months.

69. B: According to Erikson's theory of psychosocial development, the earliest stage in a child's first year of life is when s/he develops a basic sense of trust or mistrust in parents and the environment. Having their needs met sufficiently and consistently engenders trust, while having needs met inadequately and/or irregularly spawns mistrust. The second stage, in toddlerhood, involves developing a sense of autonomy or independence (A) versus one of shame and self-doubt. According to Piaget's theory of cognitive development, it is during this time period that children also develop an understanding of symbolic representation, evidenced by their engaging in make-believe or pretend play (D). According to Erikson, preschool children aged around three to five years develop a sense of initiative through exploring and exercising power over their environment, or develop a sense of guilt (C) if they garner disapproval for exerting excessive power.

70. A: It is true that conflict resolution steps have been taught successfully to children as young as eighteen months. For example, the HighScope EC curriculum, well known for its effectiveness, has sponsored the expert design of a conflict resolution approach for children aged eighteen months to six years. Conflict mediation and resolution have been taught in such settings as daycare centers, Head Start programs, preschools, nursery schools, and kindergartens. Therefore, (C) is not true. Instruction features the same steps used with adults, but adjusted commensurately with various EC developmental levels. Preschoolers are found to understand these concepts (B) when presented age appropriately. Teaching conflict mediation

and resolution to young children is found to develop lifelong social skills and problem-solving skills; hence, children *do* generalize this learning (D).

71. A: Authoritative parents are nurturing, responsive, and forgiving; they are assertive but not punitive. They make rules but explain them to children. Authoritarian (B) parents are overly strict, unresponsive, and demanding, and do not explain rules. Permissive (C) parents are nurturing, responsive, and communicative; but are also undemanding, overly indulgent, and avoid discipline. Uninvolved (D) parents are undemanding *and* unresponsive; meeting only basic child needs, they are detached from their children's lives.

72. B: Family peacemaker, clown, as well as victim, rescuer, etc., are examples of the family system component of roles. Each member's family role generalizes to school, workplace, and social settings. Boundaries (A) reflect whom and what the family includes or excludes. Rules (C) in families, spoken and unspoken, affect family life in the long term, such as planning ahead to avert problems vs. meeting these as they occur. Equilibrium (D) reflects the consistency and balance in a family.

73. C: Collectivist cultures value group harmony and cooperation, while individualist cultures value competition (A), independence (B), and uniqueness (D). World cultures that tend to espouse collectivism include Asian, Latin American, African, and Native American. Those tending to embrace individualism include North American, Canadian, European, and Australian cultures.

74. D: Assimilation is the process whereby members of one cultural group (voluntarily or involuntarily) give up their own traditions to adopt those of another culture, often one which is dominant. Acculturation (C) can mean gradual cultural modifications to a person or group through adopting some elements of another culture; the merging of cultures via long-term interaction; or a person's acquiring a society's culture from birth. Accommodation (A) as a general vocabulary word means providing a service (as in hospitality services) or adjustment (as in schools) to meet a need. As a term used by Piaget, it means forming a new schema (concept) or altering an existing one to include new input. Piaget also used assimilation (D) to mean fitting new input into an existing schema without changing the schema. Adaptation (B) in general vocabulary means adjustment; for Piaget, it meant the learning process of assimilation and accommodation combined.

75. D: Experts find that cultural competence in educational professionals is not achieved simply by hiring foreign language interpreters and translators (A), or only by hiring racially diverse personnel (B), or just by hiring educators with high self-awareness of their own cultural values (C). Rather, schools must do all three of these things; plus, the educators hired must have and/or develop the communication skills to be able to deliver effective educational services to culturally diverse children and their families, and to conduct meaningful, mutually beneficial interactions and relationships with them.

76. C: Researchers in California found that the majority of Latino parents believed their children's capacity for learning was set at birth and would not change, but that only a small minority of White parents held this belief. Hence choices (A) and (B) are incorrect. More White parents are likely to embrace transactional models of child development, seeing their children's learning as a dynamic process involving complex interactions between child and environment. This view is conducive to valuing early childhood stimulation to enhance normal learning, and early intervention to remediate developmental delays. However, the view that a child's cognitive capacity is fixed is conducive to seeing less or no benefit in early stimulation and/or intervention rather than valuing these (D), and hence to not pursuing them.

77. B: Various cultures, including African-American as an example, have strong oral traditions. Educators must take this into account rather than focusing on their not reading to their children, or reading to them less often. Telling stories and singing songs is an oral version of developing children's language skills (though it does not confer the same benefits for reading and writing language). Educators must also consider that parents who were not read to themselves as children, and grew up to succeed regardless, are unlikely to value reading to their own children (A). Educators must realize they are unlikely to influence parents whose culture does not value or prioritize reading to children (C). Educators are also unlikely to be able to teach parents to read to their children when the parents do not view children's school readiness and success as benefits of reading to them (D).

78. A: Researchers have found that parents from diverse cultures in America vary in their age expectations for many different EC developmental milestones—not just for sleeping alone (B). For instance, Anglo, Filipino, and Puerto Rican parents in the U.S. vary in the ages when they expect their children to eat solid food (C). They also have different ages when they expect their children to sleep through the night (D).

79. A: In geography, location—specifically, relative location—determines things like land prices based on the characteristics of an area, which are affected by nearby regions. An example of distance (B) is that land that is close to major highways is more expensive, while land far from main thoroughfares costs less. One example of pattern (C) in geography is that where rock folds form mountains (fold regions), the rivers accordingly form trellis patterns. Another example of pattern, in geographically oriented human behavior, is that settlements in mountainous areas form mainly spreading patterns. An example of interaction (D) in geography is when an industrial city needs raw materials from a rural village for production, and the village needs the city both as a market to buy its resources and for its industrial products: their mutual interdependence creates interaction between them.

80. B: Latitudes are lines that run east and west on geographical maps, and are also called parallels. Longitudes (A) are lines that run north and south, so longitude is not a synonym for latitude. Longitudes are also called meridians (C), so meridian is a synonym for longitude, not latitude. Coordinates (D) are the numbers of degrees assigned to various latitudes and latitudes.

81. C: A line graph makes clearest how quantities vary across periods of time, by drawing a line connecting each data point so we can see how many/much of something there was each second, minute, hour, day, week, month, year, etc. A pie chart (A) is excellent for clearly visualizing different percentages or proportions, by dividing a "pie" (circle) into "slices" representing what part of the whole each amount represents; however, pie charts do not show change across time the way line graphs do. But a bar graph (B) *can* compare quantities over time: for example, each bar could show the amount of rainfall in a given month. A column of numbers (D) is not a type of graph, and it does not make patterns and trends as clear visually as graphs do.

82. D: Teachers can use not only history books (A); they can also assign students to read well-constructed and well-written biographies (B) of famous figures in history and works of historical literature (C), which set even fictionalized stories within real historical periods and events. Historical narratives written in "storytelling" style are also good for engaging student attention while establishing chronological sequences in history.

83. C: To help young children understand citizenship concepts, teachers should help them understand the purposes and functions of laws and rules. Understanding these will help them realize that our government is made up of individuals and groups who create and enforce laws. Teachers should also help young children understand that laws limit the powers of authorities (A), preventing them from abusing their roles. Teachers should explain that laws determine the responsibilities of individual citizens (B) like themselves and their family members. They should also point out to young children that laws and rules help to make life and society more predictable, secure, and orderly (D).

Science

84. B: When young children pour sand, water, rice, etc., from one container to another, differently sized (or shaped) container, they are developing basic measurement concepts. Children fitting pegs into matching holes (A) are developing basic 1:1 correspondence concepts. Seeing how many coins they have put into their piggy bank (C) helps children develop basic counting concepts. Separating toys into piles according to type (D), color, shape, size, or any other characteristic helps children develop basic classification/categorization concepts.

85. A: When young children learn basic science concepts, an informal learning experience is defined as one wherein the child has choice and control over the activity, but at some point during the activity an adult provides some kind of intervention. When the child has complete choice and control of the activity and no adult intervenes at all (B), this is the definition of a naturalistic learning experience. If the child's activity is chosen and directed by an adult (C), or assigned to a group of children in preschool by the teacher (D), these are examples of structured learning experiences.

86. B: When scientists and students are able to identify patterns and find meaning in the results of their experiments, they are using the process skill of Inference. When they use the results of their experiments to formulate new hypotheses (A), they are using the process skill of Prediction. When they identify the properties of objects or situations using their senses, they are using the process skill of Observation. When they report the results of their experiments and their conclusions based on these results to others (D), they are using the process skill of Communication. These skills are required for solving both math and science problems.

87. C: Ammonia is known as a compound gas because its molecules contain atoms of more than one of the chemical elements—nitrogen (B) and hydrogen (D) atoms in the case of ammonia gas. Oxygen (A) as well as nitrogen and hydrogen are elementary gases rather than compound gases because their molecules contain only one chemical element.

88. D: Refraction is the process whereby the speed of light is changed as it passes from one transparent medium, like air, to another, like water. The change in speed bends the light wave. Scattering (A) is the process whereby light bounces back at multiple angles when it strikes a rough or uneven surface (instead of bouncing back at a single angle as when it strikes a smooth surface). When light bounces back off a surface, this is reflection (C). Materials that do not reflect *any* light waves (smoothly or scattered) or refract any light waves appear opaque, i.e., we cannot see through them, because they take in all frequencies of light; this is absorption (B).

89. D: Diamagnetic materials align perpendicularly to magnetic field lines, and do not retain magnetic properties when the external magnetic field is removed. These include copper, silver, gold, and most other elements in the periodic table. Paramagnetic (C) materials align parallel to magnetic field lines, and also do not retain magnetic properties upon removal of the external field. These include lithium, magnesium, molybdenum, and tantalum. Ferromagnetic (B) materials retain their magnetic properties even when the external magnetic field is removed. These include iron, nickel, and cobalt. Magnetic induction (A) is the name for the process whereby magnets turn magnetic substances near them into magnets as well.

90. C: Magnets do not have to be touching to attract or repel materials; they are able to do this from a distance. However, magnets do NOT work beyond their magnetic fields (D): the magnetic field is defined as the effective range or area of a magnet, so magnets only work within their magnetic fields by definition. Opposite poles of magnets do NOT repel (A), but instead attract each other. Conversely, the like poles of magnets do NOT attract (B), but instead repel one another.

91. B: Electricity requires a generator to make it flow. It needs a conductor as a medium through which it can travel from place to place. An insulator {(A), (C)} is a material that *blocks* the conduction of electricity. Insulation is used to prevent electricity from going where we do not want it to go—for example, into our bodies. Therefore, (D) is incorrect.

92. A: Three ways of transmitting heat are conduction (A), convection (B), and radiation (C). When heat is transmitted through solids, this is done via conduction. Conduction occurs between solid materials directly contacting one another. Convection (B) is how heat travels through liquids and gases. Heat makes them expand, lowering their density so they rise. When they cool, they recover density and fall. This heating-rising and cooling-falling process creates a current known as convection. Radiation (C), like the heat from the sun, occurs when electromagnetic waves travel through space and transfer heat to objects, like the Earth, that they touch. Therefore, (D) is incorrect.

93. B: Newton's First Law of Motion states *both* that an object at rest tends to stay at rest (A), and an object in motion tends to stay in motion (C), unless or until an opposing force changes this. Newton's *Third* Law of Motion states that for every action there is an equal and opposite reaction (D).

94. C: The most common medium in our environment that conducts sound waves, which are vibrations, is our atmosphere, i.e., the air, which is gaseous. Sound can be conducted through some solids (A) and liquids (B), but we hear sounds most often and most easily through the air. Therefore (D) is incorrect.

95. D: Sedimentary rock is formed on the surface of the earth, deposited in layers as the result of natural processes like erosion. Igneous (A) rocks are formed from volcanic eruptions. Obsidian (B) is just one type of igneous rock. Metamorphic (C) rocks form deep in the earth's crust through heavy pressure and/or heat, which metamorphose or change sedimentary and igneous rocks far below the surface.

96. C: Plants growing on land depend on sunlight to perform photosynthesis, the process whereby they convert sunlight's energy to chemical energy as fuel for their life functions. Undersea plants (A) need water and nutrients like land plants; they do not need all gases in the atmosphere but need the gases in the water, and they need less light than land plants, or no light at all, to survive. Mammals (B) need air, water, and nutrients; some mammals need more or less light, but none need light for photosynthesis as land plants do. Humans (D) are also mammals.

97. D: Human beings, like other mammals, birds, fish, reptiles, and spiders, have simple life cycles in that they are either born live or hatched from eggs, and then grow to adulthood. Frogs (A), newts (B), and grasshoppers (C) undergo metamorphoses wherein their forms change. Frogs and newts are amphibians; they begin life underwater, breathing through gills, but breathe through lungs by adulthood and move from the water to live on the land. Grasshoppers hatch from eggs into larvae, wormlike juvenile forms that do most of the feeding they need; then they progress to adulthood.

98. B: Butterflies undergo a *complete* metamorphosis during their life cycle, i.e., they completely change in form. The stages of a complete metamorphosis are (1) egg, (2) larva, (3) pupa, and (4) imago. Mosquitos (A), dragonflies (C), and grasshoppers (D) all go through an *incomplete* metamorphosis in their life cycles, including the egg, larva, and imago (adult) stages, but not the pupa stage. The butterfly pupa, called a chrysalis, is protected by a cocoon, does not feed, and is inactive until the imago (adult) emerges.

99. C: Most plants reproduce both asexually (A) and sexually (B). Asexual reproduction occurs through runners that some plants extend to root new growth, through plant cuttings being rooted in water and then planted, and through grafts. Plants reproduce sexually through fertilization, wherein plant gametes combine, contributing chromosomes from both sides, similarly to how animals mate. Since (C) is correct, (D) is incorrect.

100. B: The abiotic factors of an ecosystem are not alive; hence (A) is incorrect. Abiotic factors include such things as the atmosphere, water, soil, sunlight, temperatures, nutrient cycles, etc. While not living themselves, abiotic factors *do* affect the living organisms (C) in the ecosystem. Living organisms are biotic factors, including humans, other animals, plants, *and* microorganisms; hence abiotic factors do NOT include microorganisms (D).

Health and Physical Education

101. A: The U.S. Dept. of HHS targets obesity and tobacco use as the most preventable causes of disability and death. Alcohol use {(B), (C)} also causes disability and death but is not one of HHS' targets in the prevention initiative. (Perhaps HHS officials regard alcohol abuse as not as readily preventable.) Drug abuse (C) is also not a target of this initiative. Diabetes (D) causes disability and death; however, type 1 diabetes is genetic or organic, while type 2 diabetes is largely caused by obesity, which is a target.

102. B: Children are liable to be more vulnerable to environmental health risks than adults for several reasons. For one, children's body systems are immature and are still developing, making them easier to damage than those of adults, not vice versa (A). For another, children have smaller body sizes than adults do, so they take in more not fewer (C) toxins through the air they breathe, the water they drink, and the foods they eat. Additionally, the normal behaviors of children expose them to more, not fewer (D) toxins than normal adult behaviors do. Children are more likely to handle and mouth unsanitary and toxic substances and objects; to engage in physical contact with others having contagious illnesses; to go without washing their hands before and after using the bathroom, eating, etc.; to expose themselves unwittingly to various environmental toxins; and to lack experience and judgment about exposure.

103. C: The human skin regulates the body's temperature, and the skin is a part of the integumentary systems, which also includes the hair, nails, and sweat and oil glands. The lymphatic (A) system defends the body against infections and helps the circulatory system by returning fluids to the bloodstream. The circulatory (B) system supplies oxygen and nutrients in blood to all body tissue cells, exchanges oxygenated blood for metabolic waste products, and transports waste for elimination. The musculoskeletal (D) system provides body shape, support, stability, and locomotion, and protects the internal organs via bones and muscles. Bones also store minerals, including calcium, and the bone marrow produces blood cells.

104. D: The autonomic nervous system (A) is divided into two parts: the parasympathetic (B) and the sympathetic (C). The sympathetic part of the autonomic nervous system regulates the heartbeat. The parasympathetic part regulates muscular organ activity and glandular secretions, not heartbeat. Thus the autonomic nervous system—specifically the sympathetic part—causes our hearts to beat.

105. C: The occipital lobe, at the rear part of the brain, is associated with processing visual information. The frontal lobe (A) is associated with planning (specifically the prefrontal area), reasoning, emotions, problem solving, some parts of speech, and movement. The parietal lobe (B), between the frontal and occipital lobes, is associated with orientation, recognition and perception of stimuli, and also movement. The temporal lobe (D), below the frontal and parietal lobes, is associated with memory, speech, and the perception and recognition of auditory stimuli.

106. D: The human pancreas is an endocrine gland in that it secretes insulin, glucagon, and other hormones into the bloodstream directly without sending them through a duct. It is also an exocrine gland in that it secretes amylase, lipase, and other digestive enzymes through a duct into the digestive system (the duodenum in the small intestine). The thyroid (A) is an endocrine gland regulating weight and levels of calcium and hormones. The salivary (B) are exocrine glands that produce saliva. The pituitary (C) is an endocrine gland secreting hormones that regulate growth, blood sugar, ovarian development, fluid balances, and bonding.

107. A: Cephalocaudal means literally head-to-tail. This is the pattern of physical development for human embryos, fetuses, infants, and children. Proximodistal (B) means development from the inside out, which is also a pattern of human physical growth. (These two are not mutually exclusive but concurrent.) Mediolateral (C) is not a term generally used; but *medial* means toward the midline or closer to the inside, and *lateral* means away from the midline or closer to the outside, so "mediolateral" would have a meaning similar to proximodistal. Intellectual development (D) is like cognitive development and does not refer to patterns of motor or physical development.

108. B: When children respond to the challenges of developing increasing levels of control, coordination, speed, strength, agility, and flexibility, and achieve success, this improves their sense of self-efficacy, i.e., of how competent they are to perform and succeed at specific tasks. Children's motor skills generally develop *earlier,* not later than their language skills (A). For this reason, physical activity can offer young children a means of directly expressing themselves as much as arts activities, and before they have developed the language skills to do so (D). Physical activity develops both physical *and* cognitive skills (C) as it requires children to develop closer, more complex coordination of their mental and physical processes, as well as to develop decision-making, problem-solving, judgment, and other cognitive skills.

109. C: The NASPE's national standards for physical education include both understanding the main concepts, principles, methods, and techniques of movement and also engaging regularly in physical activity. Hence they do not exclude concepts (A). In addition to engaging in physical activity, these standards also include that an individual be able to demonstrate the motor skills (B) required for doing so. As well as valuing the physical and personal benefits of exercising, these standards moreover do include seeing value in the social benefits of physical activity (D), such as the opportunities that it offers for engaging in social interactions.

110. C: The WHO's recommendations include a *minimum* of one hour a day of moderate to vigorous physical activity for children aged five to seventeen. Therefore, a healthy youngster who engages in 15 (A) or 30 (B) minutes per day, or one hour per week (D), of physical activity does not come close to meeting this criterion. However, the recommendation also states that children can engage in either one hour of continuous physical activity, or in shorter, separate increments at different times during the day that add up to a total of one hour.

The Arts

111. B: EC teachers are advised to teach art not only in isolated lessons (A), but moreover to integrate art into the entire curriculum, which is now included in many state standards (C) for early learning and is found to improve children's understanding of many concepts and enhance their learning. Such state standards recommend integrating art projects into both individual learning units and entire curricula (C). When EC teacher assign process activities in art, they should always provide the children in advance with rules and steps (D) for proceeding, and also explain these to the children beforehand.

112. A: In addition to integrating art into the science unit and the curriculum, this activity applies artwork to build children's language skills by having them illustrate plants or animals whose names and characteristics they have learned in words; it also builds their vocabularies by having them both represent the word names and concepts of plants or animals visually, and label their

pictures with the correct word names. Activities like correctly identifying, comparing, and contrasting word names for different colors of paints, paper, and other art materials are examples of (B). Activities wherein children explore basic visual art elements by viewing and discussing artworks, and experimenting with creating their own lines, shapes, colors, and textures, are examples of (C). Activities wherein teachers ask children to make artworks showing how they feel, representing an idea, or illustrating a story are examples of (D).

113. B: The first thing the EC teacher should do when planning an art activity or project is to define which specific concept s/he wants to teach the children. With this done, the teacher should then decide what objectives s/he should fulfill in planning and implementing the activity/project (D), and identify what learning objectives s/he wants the children to meet when they participate in the activity (C). After determining these things, the teacher should then construct a simple product prototype (A). This gives the teacher an idea of the time it will take the children to make a similar product, and facilitates the teacher's determining the best order in which to sequence the activity's steps for the children.

114. C: The function of a piece of art is not unrelated to or separate from its context (A); it is necessary to know its context to determine what an artwork's function is. Context is half artist, i.e., his/her historical era, country, and social and political settings inform viewer inferences about the artist's ideas and intentions; and half viewer, i.e., what the art means to the individual viewer in his/her own time period, location, and setting informs his/her perception of and response to the work. Hence context is not dependent solely on one (B) or the other (D).

115. D: The Imagining step involves the artist's developing his or her ideas and emotions that s/he wants to express and communicate to others in his/her artwork. The second step involves (B) planning by researching, experimenting with, and designing how s/he will present the content; for example, what materials s/he will use and in what ways to achieve the effects desired. The third step entails (A) making the art product through applying artistic techniques; evaluating the product for its aesthetics, techniques, and potential effect; and refining it to optimize these. The fourth step is (C) presentation, by exhibiting visual art, or performing musical, dance, or dramatic works and performance art pieces, for audience response and participation.

116. A: As students engage in the artistic process of Creating, the teacher's introduction of other students' artworks facilitates their generalizing or transferring what they have learned about this process to the artistic process of Responding when they experience others' creations. (B) has this backward. The Analysis process involves understanding the individual components of an artwork, and seeing how they come together to appreciate the work as a whole (C); the Interpretation {(C), (D)} process involves constructing meaning from experiencing the art. The Evaluation process (D) involves assessing the quality of an artwork.

117. B: Yellow is one of the three primary colors. Primary means the color cannot be broken down into any other color, and cannot be produced by mixing other colors. Yellow, red, and blue are the primary colors. Orange (A) is a secondary color, created by mixing the primary colors yellow and red. Green (C) is a secondary color, made by mixing the primary colors blue and yellow. The secondary color purple (D) is produced by mixing the primary colors blue and red.

118. C: Pitch is the musical term meaning the frequency of the sound wave of a given musical note. Tempo (A) is the musical term meaning the relative speed of a piece of music, i.e., how slowly or quickly it should be played. Melody (B) is a tune, which is made up of a series of different pitches. Rhythm (D) is both the overall time signature of a musical piece, i.e., how many beats each measure contains, and also the patterns created by varying and repeating the durations of individual notes.

119. D: The 3/4 time signature means that there are three beats to each measure, and the quarter note equals one beat. A way to make 3/4 or waltz time easy to hear is to count, "*One* two three, *one* two three" repeatedly, stressing the first beat. 2/2 (A), or cut time, means there are two beats to each measure and the half note equals one beat. In 2/4 (B) time, there are two beats to every measure and the quarter note equals one beat. In 4/4 (C) time, there are four beats to a measure and the quarter note equals one beat. Waltz time has three counts per measure, rather than an even number (2 or 4) like the others.

120. B: While Beethoven's work included all of these organizing principles, as well as balance and unity (as great works of art generally do), the principle related specifically to its very famous and familiar main theme is repetition. The composer begins the symphony with this four-note theme and repeats it throughout—the same way, plus transposing it to different notes with the same intervals and rhythm, etc., creating striking and memorable effects while reinforcing the piece's structure.

Made in the USA
Lexington, KY
28 May 2016